The north end of Main Street in the years prior to its demolition.

Mearns Matters

by

Lesley Williams, with revisions by Anne Loudon

The shops at Mearns Cross prior to redevelopment in the 1960s, showing the offices of William Maver, builder; William N. Jamieson, chemist; J. M. Hill, newsagent; R. S. McColl, confectioner; and the City Bakeries. The premises of the Bank of Scotland are partly in view on the right.

Men in their generation are like the leaves in the trees. The wind blows and one year's leaves are scattered on the ground; but the trees burst into bud and put on fresh ones when spring comes round.

Homer

W.A.Stewart
43 Riverside Gardens
Busby
Glasgow. G76 8EP
'Phone: 0141 644 0953

The publishers regret that they cannot supply copies of any pictures featured in this book.

The authors' royalties from the sale of this book have been donated to Marie Curie Cancer Care

Contents

The view north from Mearns Cross prior to redevelopment. Pollok House is in the distance.

Acknowledgements

Miss Rae Mackinlay, Mrs J. S. Osborne, Miss E. Menzies, Mrs E. C. Dobson, Miss Bowman, Thomas L. Craig, Dr and Mrs Fordyce, Mrs Ella Cormack, Mrs Annie Lewis, Mrs Mary Dinsmor, David Arthur, James Anderson, John Anderson, Mrs Maisie Anderson, Miss Isa Russell, A. M. R. Russell, James and Marianne Deas, R. S. Barclay, Miss E. A. Calder, and the Revd W. Murray Mackay for sharing their recollections of earlier Mearns in conversation.

To Miss Marion S. McFarlane and Alasdair Morrison on whose efforts Chapter 4 largely depends; Lord James Douglas-Hamilton for permission to quote from his book on Hess; Sheriff Neil S. Gow for much of Chapter 7; Michael Moss, Glasgow University Archivist, for advice and access to the Scottish Business Archive; Janice Howie, formerly of the Eastwood District Library Local History Project, for access to her material; Mrs Marion Howie for permission to include poems by her pupils; the Greater Glasgow Health Board for text and photographs about Mearnskirk Hospital; the Glasgow Room of the Mitchell Library and Outram Press for material from *The Bulletin* and other newspapers.

And for photographs to A. M. R. Russell, Mary Dinsmor, David Arthur, Walter Clark, Mrs J. S. Osborne, Ailsa King, Anne Robertson, David Kidd, K. A. C. Melvin and Peter Cowley.

Thanks are extended to all those who helped with this new edition, and in particular: Alistair Anderson; David and Marsha Arthur; Grace Bell; Jim Carvel; John Craig; James and Marianne Deas; Maud Devine, local history librarian, East Renfrewshire Council; Susan Fisher, assistant archivist, Royal College of Physicians and Surgeons of Glasgow; Robert Grieves; Jean Harrison; Ian Hutchison; David Kidd; Paul Landman, East Renfrewshire Council; Hugh MacGilp; Gillian McKenzie; Marion Maxwell; Jim May, Greenbank Garden; Eleanor McQuade; Lynn McIntyre; members of Mearns Local History Group; Ken Melvin; Ann Morrison, Retail Trust; Stuart Nisbet; Ella Rae; the late James Raeside; Margaret Raeside; Ella Reid; John and Jean Reid; Jim Riddell; Jimmy Rodger; Andrew Russell; Sheona Stirling; Tom Stewart; Ina White; Jess Whyte.

The publishers would like to extend their thanks to all those who made pictures available for this book, particularly the Royal College of Physicians and Surgeons, Glasgow, images from whose archives appear on pages 69 and 72–78.

Foreword to the second edition

There has been increasing interest in the history of Newton Mearns since Lesley Williams published *Mearns Matters* in 1987. Despite the abundance of material which now exists, much of it relating to the social history of the area, I frequently heard expressions of regret that *Mearns Matters* was no longer available. I was delighted therefore when Stenlake Publishing agreed to produce this updated edition. It has been abridged, but contains additional material which I found of particular interest during my researches, along with a number of photographs which have not previously been published.

Lesley Williams, who lived all her life in Mearns, died prematurely in August 1990. For a spell she also worked in Mearns, where as an honours graduate in English she was a member of the teaching staff at Eastwood High School.

Despite suffering from rheumatoid arthritis from her early twenties, Lesley was an active member of the community and an

Lesley Williams, 1939–1990.

elder of Newton Mearns Parish Church. *Mearns Matters* was conceived initially when visiting Miss Rae Mackinlay in her capacity of church elder. Fascinated by Miss Mackinlay's accounts of her childhood in Mearns at the beginning of the twentieth century, Lesley realised that if these memories were not recorded they would be lost forever.

Lesley Williams was my friend from student days and was my daughter's godmother. I hope and believe that she would have been pleased to know that her book is to be republished, and I know that she would have been delighted that so many Mearns people have contributed so willingly to this new edition.

Anne Loudon, August 2003

Foreword to the first edition

Between 1931 and 1951 the population of the Parish of Mearns doubled. It has since doubled again – to 20,000 or so – as more and more people find the open country environment an attractive place to live and raise a family. Mearns Cross Shopping Centre is built over the old Main Street of the village of 'the Nitton' [Newton]. Farmlands and the policies of 'the big hooses' have given way to estates of bungalows, blocks of luxury flats, parks, schools, playing fields and golf courses. Agriculture, the traditional way of life for centuries, has almost vanished. Newton Mearns nowadays is a garden-bedecked suburb of the City of Glasgow.

Landmarks of the contemporary scene are set into their past in order to highlight how Mearns matters, and has mattered, to countless folk, both Mearns-born and incoming, throughout this century. Thus through words and images an identity is created for the 'new' Newton Mearns.

This book has been compiled with the help of many people to whom Mearns means much. Indeed only through the generous sharing of their experience has the book been possible at all. I thank them all sincerely: this is their book as much as mine. More detailed acknowledgements are made within and before the main text.

Lesley Williams, January 1987

Chapter 1

1900 . . . Garden of Eden?

In 1983, Rob Mackinlay's sister Rae recalled her early childhood in Mearns at the beginning of the century. She grew up in Firwood House:

> I remember sitting in the garden at Firwood being read a story about the Garden of Eden and my brother Rob saying, 'Yes, that'll just be something like our Mearns'.
> Firwood was built before my time, of course . . . my father built it to be ready when he married in 1891. After qualifying in medicine and sailing with the Anchor Line to India and to New York, he had settled in Mearns in 1880 . . . his father had been a doctor in Barrhead and he knew of the vacancy. Probably builders from Barrhead built the house, it's so well built . . . it had a stable and a coach-house and a hay-loft (where we children often hid) . . . two horses – one

Firwood House, Eaglesham Road.

Mearns Cross seen looking west from the Eaglesham Road. The rear of the Newton Inn is on the right, with Townhead Farm in the foreground.

would have got tired with all the hills, the Poke-hat [Pollok Halt] especially, on the way back from Barrhead . . . Barney was the name of one of them.

From the high garden of our house we looked onto green fields opposite belonging to Townhead Farm . . . the farm buildings lay behind the stables, garden and yard of the inn at the Cross. This inn faced towards Barrhead and every Friday night we could hear the music from the dance in the inn hall . . . nobody went but the farm servants, the girls in their striped petticoats and short bodices.

Townhead's fields went as far as Strangs of the Shaw Farm. We used to paddle under the road in the Mearnskirk burn above the Shaw linn. The next dwellings that way were Mr Hunter's schoolhouse at Mearnskirk and the other wee houses by the church. Across from them was the Red Lion Inn on the hill down to Thumba' Ha'.

Gilmour's fields were at the back of our house, with the farm at Fa'side. Later on an incomer, Fairweather, made it into a 'big hoose' . . . David Scott the parish minister used to say he'd never learned how long you'd to be in Mearns to become a Mearns man!

I was never a pupil at Mearns School . . . till I was eleven I went to Miss Osborne's at Broomlea, the house next to Mearns School. Three sisters, daughters of the grocer in Barrhead Road, lived there and Miss Margaret used the back parlour as the schoolroom. There were never more than two or three others. I got the three R's, piano and knitting. At eleven I went to the Girls' High in Glasgow for three years . . . walked to Eastwood Toll and took the red [tram] car, Rouken Glen/ Riddrie.

We used to go skating on the pond at Hazeldean. The Melvilles who owned Hazelden bleach and print works did silk printing and sold to Japan . . . then Japan bought the technology and eventually exports folded and they closed. The works were later demolished. Their son James was at Miss Osborne's school with my

Hazelden House.

brother and me but he was always plunking and spending the day at the smiddy of Billy Ritchie.

There was a football team, the 'Haddie heids', who always went to Nellie Crine's shop in the Main Street for hot peas and vinegar. Nellie McCabe had a dairy in the front of Burn Cottage (right on the Cross). Mr Wright, the Inspector of Poor, lived in half of it . . . tramps who wanted a night's lodging had to report to him and to my father. Then there was a woman called Mary Boyle . . . I remember being terrified just to say 'Mary Boyle' . . . maybe she was decent enough, but probably would drink. St Vigean's was the tinkers' lane – they were allowed to camp there – and at Mearns Castle . . . I was frightened for them.

My father consulted at home and had a dispensary. He'd an arrangement with the Tofts bleachworks to attend the workers in their 'woman house'. Where a row of thatched cottages stood in the Main Street, my father built a new 'land' for

Burn Cottage stood at the south-east corner of Mearns Cross next to the row of shops currently occupied by McLaren & McKechnie, opticians, and Eric N. Smith, goldsmiths.

£1,000 and feued the houses. They were called the Doctor's Buildings. I eventually sold them to a Mr Hird for £200–£300 as the rent didn't meet the factoring expenses.

Although the Doctor's Buildings were demolished with the old village Main Street in the 1960s, Dr Mackinlay's name survives in Mackinlay Place, the access road to the rear of the former Mearns Primary School and The Avenue shopping centre. For older Mearns folk, the name Mackinlay triggered off a series of affectionate memories, among them the following from Thomas Craig, who grew up on Wellmeadow Farm:

> The doctor was a conspicuous figure with striped trousers [and] a cream flowered waistcoat, double-breasted. In one of his pockets he kept a thermometer. He never carried a bag, although Nurse Deas did, but kept all the tools of his profession in one of the tails of his morning coat. He bought an Arrol–Johnston motor car when cars started to take the place of horses and he and Nurse Deas could be seen driving along about 5 m.p.h., he never changed gear from first. He was never too fond of that mode of travel and more often walked with Nurse Deas to visit patients. If we saw them on our way to school we'd say to each other, 'There's the doctor and the nurse, stand and salute'. Which one and all did.
>
> He pulled teeth in the laundry part of Firwood with the patient sitting in an old basket chair, as dentists were not even heard of in Mearns . . . no cocaine or other jags . . . just a strong arm round the neck where the hand could get the patient's jaw . . . then in went the forceps and after a struggle the patient invariably managed to get to his feet and the two did a waltz about the laundry . . . the tooth was out . . . the doctor stood triumphant with the tooth in the forceps, while the patient was down the back drive, holding his jaw, hearing the doctor call, 'It's out. I have it here'.

Nurse Deas (Bella Logie, d. 1948) was the village nurse. She worked with both Dr Mackinlay and his successor, Dr Fordyce. Kind but firm, she was much respected and had a wealth of experience. Dr Mackinlay's family home, The Firs or Firwood, continues to command an extensive view in Eaglesham Road; nowadays, however, of gardens and rooftops rather than open fields and farms. And still from Mearns Cross (albeit no longer a crossroads since Asda was built and the roads were realigned), past Firwood eastwards, the road winds up and down to Mearns Kirk, the crowning landmark of what was once a country parish of farms, moorland, village, and the occasional country house.

Nurse Deas.

Chapter 2

Most Gladsome Parish – Kirk, Cattle, Countryside and Covenanters

The original centre of the parish was not at Mearns Cross, as one might have expected, but at Mearnskirk. There inn, school, rows of cottages and smiddy clustered along the ridge crowned by the kirk of the parish. The present church building dates from 1813. Legend, however, associates a Celtic church of St Bride with the site. Records show that in the Middle Ages money was sent to Paisley Abbey; indeed legend has it that *all* the kirk money went to Paisley in return for the monks there saying prayers for the souls of the Mearns dead. Thus, the kirk at Mearns was perpetually impoverished. Be that as it may, congregations have worshipped there since pre-Reformation times.

Stones in the graveyard date from 1742, one of the best preserved of which is the horizontal memorial to the ministry of the Revd Dr McLatchie. He was ordained assistant to the Revd Alexander Cruikshank on 11 April 1786 and succeeded him in 1791. In March 1824 he himself was succeeded by the Revd Donald MacKellar.

To Dr McLatchie, an incomer over 200 years ago, fell the duty of contributing with all the other parish ministers in Scotland to the *Statistical Account of Scotland*. This is the earliest extended writing which describes the district. Under the editorship of Sir John Sinclair, 21 volumes describing every shire in Scotland were published between 1791 and 1799. The account was subtitled 'an enquiry into the country for the purpose of ascertaining the quantum of happiness enjoyed by its inhabitants and the means of its future improvement'. Dr McLatchie had a high regard for his parishioners, describing them thus:

> The people of this parish are sober, industrious, and economical; respectful to their superiors and uncommonly friendly and obliging.
>
> They are rational in their religious sentiments and moderate in their religious zeal. All of them are strongly attached to our present civil constitution and cautiously avoid giving countenance to any change or innovation in it. It is happy for them that they pretend not to make politics their study. They mind the duties and business of their own station, and wish to enjoy with thankfulness and peace the many blessings which a kind providence bestows on them.

Mearns Kirk. The small square building was the original session house.

The pipe band of the 138th Glasgow Company Boys' Brigade photographed on Armistice Day in the late 1940s. Taught by Mr Wm. Stewart (left foreground), the boys met for practice in the old session house which then contained a fireplace. In the days of national coal shortage following the Second World War, each boy had to bring a lump of coal to band practice for the fire.

Born in 1757, Dr McLatchie was nineteen when the American colonists declared their independence from the Britain of King George III, and 32 when the fall of the Bastille heralded the French Revolution. He came to Mearns in 1786 and may well have been writing his account of the parish when King Louis XVI and Queen Marie Antoinette were executed in 1792 with many of the French aristocracy. He was pleased, therefore, to observe no radical tendencies among his flock. Mearns has perhaps a long history of conservatism!

Between 1834 and 1845 the *New Statistical Account* was compiled in which Mr MacKellar, Dr McLatchie's successor, contributed the information about the Parish of Mearns, completing his work in January 1842. He too was pleased with the character of the inhabitants:

> As this is strictly a rural district, the people are characterised to a certain extent by simplicity of manners and by an absence of many of the vices that are more common and more fashionable in populous manufacturing districts.

Both ministers help form a picture of the rural Mearns of earlier days. Dairying predominated:

> The soil is all of a light and quick kind . . . chiefly remarkable for its fine pasture. It produces grass both in greater quantity than common and likewise of the very best kinds, and it everywhere abounds with a profusion of white clover. The greater part of the land is in pasturage.
>
> Every farm is stocked with milk cows; and the principal object of the farmer is to produce butter, and butter-milk, for the Glasgow market. The butter that is made here, and especially that which is salted for winter use, is reckoned preferable to any other and the demand for it is vastly greater than can be answered. It has nothing of that rancid taste which butter made on deeper and heavier soils is sometimes found to have; and it keeps in good condition for a very long time.
>
> The churning of milk makes a great and laborious part of the farmers' work. Of late they have introduced the use of churning-mills driven by water. There are many streams which run through the parish and answer for these mills and, on trial, they prove highly beneficial and save a great deal of labour. (*Statistical Account of Scotland.*)

> The dairy cows are all of the Ayrshire breed, are finely formed, and of the best sort. Butter and butter-milk are here manufactured in a style not surpassed in any other district in the west of Scotland. The Mearns butter is famed in Glasgow and Paisley and families are anxious to lay in their winter butter, the veritable produce of the celebrated dairies of the Mearns. (*New Statistical Account of Scotland.*)

Not surprisingly, one of the social highlights of the rural Mearns calendar was the annual cattle show, held by Mearns Agricultural Society on the last Saturday of April 'at 11 o'clock prompt'. The 1919 show had 24 classes for Ayrshire cattle: fourteen for milk stock and ten for bulls and yeld stock. There were fourteen classes for Clydesdale horses and a further seven horse classes, along with sheep classes for Leicesters, blackfaced and crossbreeds. Fourteen poultry classes were included, and there were also prizes for best collie dog.

Sisters Lizzie and Jessie Harvie of Waterside Farm in their working clothes.

Lizzie and Jessie Harvie photographed on 26 June 1899.

Waterside Farm, 1930s.

Mearns Cattle Show, 1932, showing Morag Lambie with her uncle Alec Lambie admiring Robert Harvie's champion Ayrshire cow from Waterside Farm.

1925.	Expenditure.		
Nov 11	Price of Crofthead, Newton Mearns.	3,400	
Nov. 11	Outlays on recording disposition.	50. 8.	
18.	Set of plough-backbands & chains	2. 3	
18.	Hedge knife.	5	6.
30.	Rake & Fork.	5	
1926.			
Jan. 28.	One horse.	35.	
" 8.	One cart	28	
Feb. 10	Two pairs of plough hames & straps.	1	7 6.
" 12.	2 pails, 1 white wash brush & 2½ sts. lime	10.	
" 13.	Part insurance of Farm	1 14 3.	
14.	Stall Collar	1	9.
24.	1 set Diamond Harrows	4 10	
		3,544	7.

Page from William Riddell's account book detailing his purchase of Crofthead Farm in 1925. The Mearnscroft housing development was built around the farmhouse.

Teeny Brown from Cheapside Street, Eaglesham, was a dairymaid at Loganswell Farm. She is pictured with her milk bine, butter search and spade (left), and a butter churn (right). A bine was a shallow basin of large diameter from which the cream was skimmed off milk.

Robert Raeside (born 1925) ploughing at Maidenhill Farm in the early 1950s.

A younger Robert Raeside with a mare in foal.

Agnes, Jeanie and Janet, daughters of James Watson of Langlee Farm, photographed c.1918. James Watson farmed Langlee from 1893 to 1924.

There were categories for best oatcakes, soda scones, potato scones, pancakes, shortbread and jelly sponge. Milking competitions were held for seniors (any age) and juniors (fourteen years and under) for the 'Quickest and Best Milker. Competitors provide own Cow which must give at least 12 lbs of milk at Milking'. Cash prizes were usually awarded, but depending on the allocation of the many donations in kind, other prizes might be won. For instance a felt hat (valued at a guinea), donated by Kirsops, was won by the competitor showing the best Leicester. Other unusual prizes in 1919 included a pair of slippers, roast beef worth £1 and a box of soap.

'Luncheon', from 1 to 2.15 p.m., was the focus of the day for all self-respecting and proper participants. A full-page notice in the prize list reminded members of their social obligations, namely that 'competitors gaining more than 10/- prize money will require to dine or forfeit 5/-; this penalty will be enforced'. The lunch was held in the Unionist Rooms in Barrhead Road and the advert noted that visitors could reach Mearns by 'Train from Central Station, Glasgow, to Giffnock and Whitecraigs. Motor Buses to and from Mearns will run at intervals between the car terminus [i.e. the tram terminus at Eastwood Toll] and Giffnock and Whitecraigs Railway Stations, during the day.' Those who could not afford it or did not qualify for the official luncheon bought pies at Hay's the baker in Barrhead Road. Demand was such that:

> The week before the show my father had to employ an extra baker from Glasgow –
> he lodged for the week in Ashview Terrace – and from about four o'clock every
> morning right through the day we made hundreds and hundreds of twopenny pies
> (meat from Johnson's) and tarts. All the farmer people bought them – to eat them
> and to take away – 'I'll just pick up a couple of dozen on the way home from the
> show', they'd say.

The show itself was held 'on Mr Gilmour's Field adjoining Newton Mearns', an easy walk from the Unionist Rooms where lunch was served. 387 separately itemised donations funded the 1919 show. Most donors gave five shillings, ten shillings or one guinea, in return for which they could compete in the show and read their name on the donors' list. Mrs Mather of Kirkhill House and Mr Hannay of The Broom each gave £1, more or less the going 'big house' rate. All in all the patrons contributed £204, 11s., 6d. That year 21 gifts were received, some of which have already been mentioned as prizes in the Ayrshire classes. Others included a silver fern pot, a steel graip (an iron pronged fork used in farming and gardening), a £6 chest of finest tea, two whips and an umbrella. Admission charges increased the revenue – one shilling for adults and sixpence for juveniles – a lot of money in those days. Enterprising youngsters of course found other ways in. Village families all enjoyed the spectacle of the fully dressed Clydesdales as they passed along Main Street on their way to the show field.

Opposite:

John Lammie, William Raeside, Finlay Cunningham, George Watson and Robert Raeside Snr. cut corn and gather the sheaves into stooks to dry at the Star and Garter Farm.

Agnes Watson at Langlee Farm with her luggie (a pail used for milking).

Jimmy McIntyre collecting milk for the creamery at Ryat Farm in the 1960s, photographed with Laddie, the farm dog.

What a great day the cattle show was . . . in the morning the clip clop of the big horses – the Clydesdales – their tails all tied up – along the Main Street . . . the houses were all cleaned and whitewashed for the cattle show . . . then the cows . . . and the hens . . . everyone came in from all around for the shows at night – Christmas was nothing compared to it.

Agriculture in Mearns had reached a very sophisticated level in the 100 years since Dr McLatchie and Mr MacKellar were praising its butter production, and greater changes were not far away. Let's return, however, to the days of Dr McLatchie, author of the first *Statistical Account* in the 1790s, to savour a little more of a way of life that was soon to vanish in the face of the growth of Glasgow. (The church and school referred to below were those at Mearnskirk. Dr McLatchie's church was replaced in 1813 by the present Mearns Parish Kirk. The parish school at Mearnskirk stood on the site of the present manse.)

Poor – There are but few poor in the parish. These are supported in the usual way; by collections made at the church, by the interest of a small accumulated fund, by the profits of the mortcloth, and by dues arising from the publication of the banns of marriage. There are no begging poor belonging to the parish. [A mortcloth was a pall which covered a coffin on its way to the grave, latterly chiefly hired out by the kirk session. Funds collected from the hire of the mortcloth were used to alleviate the poor of a parish.]

School – There is a parochial schoolmaster who has a salary of £8.6s.8d sterling besides the usual small school fees and an allowance of 30s as Session Clerk. There is the same reason to complain here, as in most other places, that the emoluments of the schoolmaster are in no way adequate to the qualifications expected and to the labour and fatigue required.

Church – Sir Michael Stewart of Blackhall, Bart. is patron. The stipend is five chalders of meal, and £27.13s sterling of money. No augmentation has ever yet been demanded. The glebe consists of about four acres of arable land. A very good manse was built in 1789 and the church was fitted up in a very neat and commodious manner in 1792.

There has long been an Anti-burgher meeting-house here. The

Mrs Janet Harvie (née Ballantine, 1863–1952) was one of the last pupils to attend the Parish School at Mearnskirk, walking there from Craigend Farm near Patterton via the village of Newton. It is said that on a Sunday she walked the same route to church at Mearnskirk, stopping to wash her feet in the burn at the bottom of the glebe and to change her shoes and stockings.

Mearns Parish Church and the Glebe from the Mearnskirk Road (now Eaglesham Road).

The building in the right foreground of this view looking north along Main Street was the first manse of the Secession Church; the smaller structure beyond it was the church itself, which had become a shop by this time.

congregation, which is not near so numerous now as formerly, is made up of people belonging to this parish and to some of the adjoining parishes.

There are likewise in the parish a few Burghers and Cameronians. It is pleasant to see the happy effects of toleration. Time has softened the rancour of party among these seceders from the Established Church, and almost all of them live in good neighbourhood and discover a spirit of Christian charity and moderation.

The Anti-burgher meeting house referred to was the first church of the congregation from which the present Newton Mearns Parish Church was established. It was situated in the Main Street and latterly became J. Elliott's grocer's shop.

Christopher North

To Dr McLatchie's 'very good manse' – doubtless a happy supplement to his stipend of 'five chalders of meal and £27.13s sterling of money' – came young men to prepare for entrance to university.

Among his boarders was John Wilson of Paisley (1785–1854), who after studying at Glasgow University and Magdalen College, Oxford became Professor of Moral Philosophy at Edinburgh University. Those were the days when Edinburgh was styled the Athens of the North. Under the nom de plume of Christopher North, Professor Wilson became famous throughout Britain through the satirical articles he contributed to *Blackwood's Magazine*.

Mr Wilson senior, a Paisley merchant, had chosen to send his son to Dr McLatchie's manse to ensure a sound classical education in the healthy moorland environment of the Mearns. John Wilson later nostalgically recalled his boyhood haunts in a collection of autobiographical essays called *Recreations of Christopher North*, most notably in the essays entitled 'Our Parish' and 'May Day' (1842). He referred to Mearns as 'the cheerfullest and most gladsome parish in all ... Scotland', going on describe it as 'neither highland or lowland – but undulating like the sea in the sunset after a day of storms'.

Fishing was a frequent pastime with the young scholars: 'The best beloved, if not the most beautiful, of all the lochs was the Brother Loch ... tradition assigned the name on account of three brothers that perished in its waters'. Christopher North went on to portray a highlight of the local social calendar:

The Brother Loch saw annually another sight, when on Green Brae was pitched a tent – a snow-white pyramid gathering to itself all the sunshine.

There lords and ladies and knights and squires celebrated old May-Day and half the parish flocked to the festival.

The Earl of Eglintoun, and Sir Michael Shaw-Stewart and old Sir John of Polloc, and Pollock of that ilk, and other heads of illustrious houses – with their wives and daughters, a beautiful show – did not disdain them of low degree but kept open table on the moor; and, would you believe it, high born youths and maidens ministered at the board to cottage lads and lasses, whose sunburned faces hardly dared to smile under awe of that courtesy – yet whenever they looked up there was happiness in their eyes.

The young ladies were all arrayed in green; and after the feast they took bows and arrows in their lily hands and shot at a target in a style that would have gladdened the heart of Maid Marion – nay of Robin himself.

Christopher North is attributed in the *Oxford Dictionary of Quotations* with the saying 'Laws are made to be broken', and is said to have written the words of the song *Turn Ye to Me*. He seems to have been a larger-than-life character, for he was described by friends as 'a sixteen stoner, a cocker, a racer, a six bottler, a twenty-four tumbler, an out and outer, a true, upright, knocking down, poetical, prosaic, moral, professional, hard-drinking, fierce-eating, good-looking, honourable and straightforward Tory'. Ludovic Kennedy is his great-great-great-grandson.

Mearns Parish Kirk

Mearns Parish Kirk enjoys a commanding site and is visible throughout the parish it serves. The gateposts at the entry to the kirkyard are hollow with room inside for a sentry. In the days when there was reputed to be a market with anatomists for cadavers, relatives of the recently deceased, armed with cudgels, or even blunderbusses, stood there to protect the newly buried body. Perhaps West of Scotland admirers of Burke and Hare made body-snatching raids on Mearns kirkyard. The Anatomy Act of 1832 ended such worries.

In the earlier years of the twentieth century hot pies and glasses of porter were served at the Red Lion Inn to parishioners who walked or rode to morning worship from a distance and who often stayed over the 'interval' for a further service in the afternoon. Horses could be stabled in the inn yard. A pail of water and a drinking cup stood by the church gateway beside the collection plate to refresh those dry from their walk up to the kirk.

The present phosphor bronze weathercock weighs 2½ cwt. (about 125 kg) and was set atop the steeple shortly after the Second World War. It replaced an earlier bird which had lost part of its tail years before when two shooting patrons from the Red Lion hit their target. While a prisoner of war the Revd Drummond Duff (minister from 1929 to 1951)

The chimneys of the Red Lion Inn at Mearnskirk can just be seen behind the smoke of the steam road roller. The sign in the foreground reads BEWARE ROAD ROLLER AT WORK. Kirkview Crescent now occupies the approximate site of the Red Lion.

was promised by a fellow prisoner, Captain Holm of Hazelden, that if they both survived he would present the church with a new weathercock as a thank-offering.

Dr McLatchie commented that his church was 'fitted up in a very neat and commodious manner'. He would find equal pleasure in the current church. In 1931 and 1932 the interior was wholly renovated and the present chancel built out from the north wall. The plain glass windows on the south wall were replaced by stained glass, one depicting the disciple Andrew and the other Queen Margaret, patron saint of the Church in Scotland. Many lovely windows have been added since. The present organ was installed following an appeal launched in 1982 to celebrate the jubilee of the renovation. Further alterations and improvements to the church building were completed in the year 2001. A new main entrance was formed in the east gable and a raised floor in the chancel was extended into the nave. Facilities for the disabled were installed and improvements to the amplification system were made.

Following the Second World War a modern manse and new halls were built within the four acre glebe. The previous manse, situated diagonally opposite at the corner of Humbie Road, has been divided into flats and three smaller houses share its grounds. Present-day ministers would not have room to board boys studying for university as Dr McLatchie did (nor space for domestic staff!). The new halls were officially opened by Miss C. W. Ritchie on 8 January 1971, after which the old hall (built in 1910 and located on Ayr Road opposite the former Mearns Primary School) was sold to the Jewish community. It has recently been upgraded and extended, and is now called the Glasgow New Synagogue Centre. Miss Ritchie (1884–1975), daughter of blacksmith Billy Ritchie, was a well-known and respected teacher at Mearns School. She was first a pupil, later a pupil-teacher and latterly infant mistress from 1926 until her retiral in 1946.

Red Lion Inn, Newton Mearns

Newton Mearns Parish Church

Dr McLatchie recognised that even in his days of fairly universal churchgoing not all the people of the parish attended his church, and he alluded to an Anti-burgher meeting house and other seceding groups. Newton Mearns Parish Church traces its origins to this seceder tradition. During the eighteenth century the Anti-burgher meeting houses or churches in Main Street drew their congregations from as far off as Neilston and Eaglesham. 1836 saw the opening of a church large enough to seat 400, which became part of the United Presbyterian Church from 1847 (this subsequently became the United Free Church of Scotland, then united with the Church of Scotland in 1929). Among its Communion plate is a pewter paten stamped with a ship in full sail squarely bordered with the words 'Success to the United States of America', serving as a reminder that many of those who dissented from the practices of the established churches in Scotland and England chose to cross the Atlantic to seek freedom of worship. When the custom of a precentor leading the praise gave way to the use of an organ at the Secession Church, it is said that a Malletsheugh worthy who had attended church every Sunday of his long life promptly stopped coming, declaring that the organ was a 'kist of whustles'!

The Revd A. Boyd Scott was minister of Newton Mearns Parish Church from 1901 to 1903 and wrote *Old Days and Ways in Newton Mearns* in 1938 to celebrate the bicentenary of the church. The longest Mearns ministry of the twentieth century was that of the Revd W. Murray Mackay who served Newton Mearns Parish Church from 1931 to 1976. As a young minister one of his first tasks was to oversee the building of the present church at Mearns Cross. On 10 December 1938 Mrs Templeton of Crookfur laid the memorial stone

The church of 1836, which was demolished in 1938 and replaced by the present Newton Mearns Parish Church.

Revd A. Boyd Scott.

Newton Mearns Parish Church under construction in 1938.

David Arthur (with pipe in mouth), beadle of Mearns Kirk, photographed with his family at Mearnskirk. The former Mearns Parish School is on the left.

and a year later the dedication service was conducted. Masonry from the previous church was used in the internal walls, and stones dated 1743 and 1754 from earlier church buildings were incorporated into the vestibule. A bell tower was one of the gifts of the Young family in memory of their son Robert who was killed in the Second World War.

A long ministry like Mr Mackay's has been by no means unique in the annals of the Newton Mearns congregation. The first two ministers – Andrew Thomson, father and son – served from 1746 until 1816. Originally a Praying Society, the congregation itself dates from 1738 and built its first church in 1743. Andrew Thomson Snr was ordained in the church on 26 March 1746, three weeks before the Battle of Culloden.

Robert Pollok and Mearns Parish School

One of the children baptised in 1798 by Andrew Thomson Jnr. was Robert Pollok. A century ago the fame of this young poet, who died in 1827 in his 29th year, was quite remarkable. Now he is unknown, even within his own parish. His fame rested on an epic poem, *The Course of Time*, running to 300 pages. Published in Edinburgh in 1827 it won great critical acclaim, one London reviewer even ranking Pollok 'in the good company of Dante and Milton'. Within 40 years of his death over 78,000 copies had been sold. Among Robert Pollok's earlier writings were stories about the Covenanters, set on the moors where he was raised. For six years he walked from Mid Moorhouse Farm (south of Eastwood Golf

Club) to Mearns Parish School, then at Mearnskirk. The teaching there was described favourably by Mr MacKellar in his 1842 contribution to the *New Statistical Account*:

> The parish school-room is one of the largest and airiest of any in the west of Scotland. Mr Jackson, the very able and excellent teacher, has long laboured with much success in his very important and useful sphere as parochial teacher. According to the last official returns, the number of children attending the parish school was 103, attending other schools, 150. The branches taught in the parish school are Latin, geography, arithmetic, English grammar, reading and writing. The salary of the parochial teacher is £34.4s., school-fees £63, with £4 annually from other sources. There is a school at Busby and a small country school besides. There are few, if any, natives above fifteen years of age who cannot read the Scriptures, and who have not been taught to write.

From Mr Jackson's tutelage Robert and his elder brother David transferred to Fenwick where a Mr John Fairlie advanced their Latin studies in preparation for entry to Glasgow University. During the school week the boys boarded with an uncle at Horsehill, Fenwick, and according to David in his *Life of Robert Pollok*, it was while walking the eight miles between Mid Moorhouse and Horsehill that Robert began composing poetry in his head.

Like his mentor Milton, Robert Pollok did not at first aspire to be a full-time writer. His university studies were directed towards the ministry and he became licensed as a preacher of the United Secession Church. Ill-health prevented his seeking a charge. Following the publication of *The Course of Time* well-wishers contributed to his wintering in Italy, whither he sailed from Leith with his sister in September 1827. He died en route and is buried in Southampton.

Throughout the nineteenth century Pollok's work was held in high esteem and his birthplace at Moorhouse was on the itinerary of many a walker from Glasgow. One such was Hugh Macdonald of 62 John Street, Bridgeton. In 1854 as 'Caleb' of the *Glasgow Citizen* he published 21 'Rambles Round Glasgow, with a resumé of the Historical, Biographical and Traditional associations of the various localities'. In the ninth of these he joined Robert Pollok's brother David for a walk from Waterfoot up the River Earn to the Moorhouses and beyond:

> Passing Humbie Brig and the fine farm of Titwood, we soon arrive at the bleach works of Hazelden, where we cross to the south or Eaglesham side of the Earn. A few minutes' walk further, during which we pass Hazelden Head, Hazelden Mains, and various other places with Hazelden prefixes, brings us to the lands of North Moorhouse, the birthplace of Robert Pollok the gifted author of *The Course of Time*.

In the heyday of tramcars 70 years later, Glasgow Corporation Transport Department featured the Moorhouse area in its official guide to the 'Romantic and Beautiful Countryside Around the City'. T. C. F. Brotchie was the author and artist of this 1920 guide. He walked the five or six miles from the tram terminus at Clarkston Toll (fare from Jamaica Street threepence) and sketched North Moorhouse Farm where Pollok had been born. The lines from Pollok's verse which Brotchie quoted describe trees at Mid Moorhouse where the poet lived from his seventh year.

Tall trees they were
And old and had been old a century
Before my day. None living could say aught
About their youth; but they were goodly trees,
And oft I wondered as I sat and thought
Beneath their summer shade, or in the night
Of winter heard the spirits of the wind
Growling among their boughs, how they had grown
So high in such a rough tempestuous place.

Only two of Pollok's tall trees remained in that 'rough tempestuous place'. Brotchie saw a 'windswept solitary spot, 830 feet above sea level and exposed to every wind that blows – a forgotten, neglected spot now little more than a gable end'.

A monument to the poet, commissioned to celebrate the centenary of his birth, was unveiled on 24 September 1900. The granite memorial with its bronze medallion stands at Loganswell at the junction of the A77 and Mearns Road, and bears this eloquent tribute to Robert Pollok: 'He soared untrodden heights and seemed at home'. When the monument was erected a volume of his poetry was placed under it along with some coins minted that year. A car knocked over the memorial *c*.1980 and these items were retrieved, although the book was badly water-damaged.

New Roads and Visitors

Caleb in the 1850s and Brotchie in the 1920s are representative of the many walkers who sought a change from the smoky industrial city of Glasgow to the fresh moorland air of upland Mearns. For their further refreshment a new institution was established – the tearoom. There were two at Mearns Cross – the Neuk and the Bungalow – while at Loganswell there was the Red House. Two more were located at Hazelden, one each at Pilmuir, Malletsheugh and Patterton. Nearby farms found a new market for their eggs with parties of ramblers booking in for ham and egg teas on Saturday evenings.

The Bungalow Tearoom on the Kilmarnock Road (now Ayr Road).

The original Malletsheugh Inn, built in 1842 with stone from the Giffnock quarries.

Previously travellers had depended upon the old coaching inns – the Red Lion, Star and Garter, Turf, Kingswell, Newton and Malletsheugh. Of these only the Malletsheugh remains, although now in its third premises, the second having burned down. Until 1832 the north/ south routes through the district followed the line of the present Stewarton Road from Spiersbridge or ran via Clarkston, Mearnskirk, Loganswell, the Floaks and on to Fenwick. This latter route became known as the 'Old Line' after the construction of a 'New Line' (the present A77) from Giffnock via Mearns Cross to Loganswell and beyond. This new road contributed to the shift in the centre of parish life from Mearnskirk to the village of the Newton. The Star and Garter Inn on the Old Line between Loganswell and Mearnskirk closed and became a farm. It is now a private house. Improved road surfaces along with the later inventions of the bicycle, the pneumatic tyre and the internal combustion engine gradually led to swifter communication between Mearns and Glasgow. This radically changed the area. What was once a rural parish of scattered fermtouns and a two-street village where people lived and worked began the transition to a suburb, most of whose residents now commute to work in Glasgow.

The New Line was originally maintained by tolls collected at Eastwood Toll, Loganswell and the Floaks. A vehicle drawn by six horses was charged four shillings Scots (four pence English), the levy being reduced if fewer horses were used. Cattle passed the toll at tenpence per score (twenty). Sledges – which may have been used in muddy conditions as well as in icy or snowy weather – paid four and a half pence. A horse, laden or otherwise, paid threepence toll if not drawing a vehicle. Carts carrying materials for building and paving Glasgow streets paid no tolls. The system of charging tolls was introduced in 1750, and revenue for the maintenance of the roads was derived from these for many years afterwards. They were abolished on the New Line in the mid-1880s.

This photograph of Eastwood Toll (showing the tollhouse of 1832) was taken by John Crawford, who frequently included his bicycle in his compositions.

After a spell as Nellie Niven's sweetie shop, Eastwood tollhouse (known locally as Nellie's Toll) was demolished *c.*1907, while Loganswell stood until the middle of the twentieth century. Beyond the Loganswell tollhouse, with its little shop at the front, was Loganswell School which survived until 1928 when the sole teacher, Mrs Bell, was transferred to Mearns along with her seven pupils. An anecdote from a former Loganswell pupil highlights the quietness of even the main roads in those days:

> Mrs Stewart was absent once – during the Spanish flu' epidemic at the end of the war, I think it was – and Miss Maver came up daily from Mearns School . . . she came by cab driven by Johnny Cannon in his tile hat. One time we hurled the blackboard out into the middle of the road and Minnie Ross was playing at being teacher – she was the wildest girl that ever was – I was the 'watcher' for Johnny Cannon's hat coming round the corner.

The speed of the approaching cab easily permitted a successful withdrawal of the blackboard before Miss Maver made her entry!

The pace of life in the early days of the twentieth century had changed little in hundreds of years, and prior to today's heavy volume of fast-flowing traffic the highways and byways around Mearns were a pleasure to walk and cycle. Returning to Caleb as an example, from Moorhouse he continued his walk southwards and upwards to where the River Earn is formed by the confluence of the burns from the Floaks with the burn from Black Loch.

We are now at the head of the vale and in the very heart of the Mearns Moor.

Around us on every side a dreary expanse of brown heathy hills and dark morasses stretches away to the horizon. Here and there a few comparatively fertile spots enliven the waste; each with a cluster of ash trees and a little wreath of blue smoke marking the sites of the thin strewn pastoral farms.

Yet there is a peculiar beauty in the wild landscape, all black and dreary as it is . . . the peesweep flutters round our head and the snipe starts from our path on its tortuous flight, while at our feet we have the meeting of the waters which form the lovely Earn . . . there is a pleasing harmony in the music of their many waters.

Covenanters

The moors were not always as still and desolate as Caleb found them. In common with north Ayrshire and west Lanarkshire, the moorlands of east Renfrewshire are steeped in the legends and history of the Covenanters. The triangle bounded by Mearns, Eaglesham and Fenwick is Covenanting heartland, and at the Floaks on the East Renfrewshire/East Ayrshire boundary the Covenanting Captain John Paton was captured and in May 1684 hanged in the Grassmarket in Edinburgh.

As an impecunious student, lodged in a Crown Street tenement while at Glasgow University, Robert Pollok published his first writings to help make ends meet. These were three tales of the Covenanters: *The Persecuted Family*, *Ralph Gemmill* and *Ellen of the Glen*. One of his source books would have been John Howie's biography *The Scots Worthies*, which from its appearance in 1775 became a standard work on the subject of the Scottish Covenant. Howie farmed at Lochgoin where conventicles were so frequent in his great-grandparents' days that it was raided twelve times. A tall granite obelisk commemorating Howie and the famous men whose lives he recounted has stood since 1896 near Lochgoin Farm at the point where Covenanting guards kept a lookout for the troopers. On their warning, the household and any fugitives would flee to the safety of the bogs which stretched for miles behind the farmhouse.

At a conventicle on 23 July 1967, convened in the shadow of the monument, the late Lord Rowallan gifted Lochgoin Farm to the Fenwick and Lochgoin Covenanters' Trust. A small museum is maintained within the farmhouse which is easily reached by car. The single-track access road is clearly signed off the B764 Eaglesham road about one and a half miles north of its junction with the A77. Among the exhibits are Captain Paton's sword and the Howie family tree, spanning nine centuries.

Country Postmen

Lochgoin links with Fenwick and Eaglesham rather than Mearns. The neighbouring farms of Highfield and Shieldhill, however, mark the south-eastern extremity of one of Mearns early postal walking routes. Six days a week, in all weathers

a nippy wee man, Tommy McMeechin, left the village before 7 a.m. . . . fully loaded [with] puttees on his legs . . . and went off up the Eaglesham Road, past the houses at Mearnskirk, past Billy Ritchie's smiddy, to Eastfield, Southfield, Westfield, the Hazeldens, Crook, the Star, Broadlees; down to Muirshiel on the Earn; up to the Moorhouses, Langlee, the Bennan; across the fields to Shieldhill; then half an hour at Highfield for a cup of tea; across the fields again, down and up to the Floaks,

Barcapel flats were built on the site of Barcapel House after it was destroyed by fire in 1965.

and on up to High Cairn; down via Low Cairn and Brownside, reaching Loganswell and his last call at Greenhags (now the East Renfrewshire Council coup) by midday whence back to do a bit of tailoring in the afternoon.

There were no days off for Christmas or New Year, and on New Year's Day Tommy reached Greenhags about 6 p.m., often with icicles on his beard but warmed by a few more 'teas' than his usual one cup at Highfield. A cursory look at the map suggests that Tommy's round – which covered rough and hilly terrain – was probably about eleven miles long, an impressive journey to make on foot in five hours.

This tailoring postie was succeeded by Bertie Crawford from Malletsheugh cottages. He 'sang all the time' and also covered the hilly round on foot. A bike was of little use for short cuts across the fields and burns. A cycling postie on the Capelrig / Barcapel / Patterton route used to interrupt his deliveries to lay snares, the postbag being handy for bringing back the rabbits caught. Singing, hunting, and tailoring postmen sadly disappeared with the introduction of vans in the 1930s.

In the days before broadcasting, when country families read weekly rather than daily newspapers, immediate happenings and urgent communications came through neighbours, children, the postman, itinerant salesmen and tramps. The Lammies of Greenhags heard of the outbreak of the First World War from a tramp at their back door who knew his statement – 'The war has broken oot' – would be good for something to eat in exchange.

Most of the farmland has now gone – for housing estates and other purposes – and many of the farmhouses and steadings have been demolished or converted into suburban houses. Changed or gone are most of the burns and hedgerows. On a more positive note, although afforestation has begun at the East Renfrewshire/East Ayrshire boundary, most of the moorland of Christopher North's 'most gladsome parish' remains much as it has been for centuries.

A. Guthrie Wren was the proprietor of the Newton Mearns Inn (also known as Porter's Inn) when this picture was taken.

A postcard of the Main Street written on 22 May 1916 and franked at Newton Mearns post office. Prospect House can be seen in the distance.

Chapter 3

Village Life and Work

The principal village in the parish is Newtown, situated about half a mile north west from the parish church. It is a burgh of barony, and has the right of holding a weekly market, and two annual fairs. It contains about 500 or 600 inhabitants, and is formed chiefly of two rows of houses on the Glasgow and Ayrshire road, with a good Inn.

So wrote the Revd MacKellar in the *New Statistical Account*. 100 years later, in 1939, the Revd Boyd Scott wrote in *Old Days and Ways in Newton Mearns*:

Mearns has lost its isolation; and the village of Newtown is now little more than a grey smudge upon the great red-roofed suburbia that has appeared above ground like a coral reef above the green sea.

A generation later and this 'grey smudge' itself had gone. Post-war neglect culminated in demolition of the old village in the sixties, and apart from a dwindling store of memories the only trace of it that remains is a single tree. Situated on the access road to The Avenue, this previously marked the spot where the back garden of the Doctor's Buildings met the old school playground. Though greatly regretted by many of its inhabitants, the passing of the Newton village may have been somewhat less lamented by the country folk of the parish if the remarks of two Loganswell residents (who were octogenarians when the first edition of this book was published in 1987) are anything to go by: they described the village as 'jist a wee footerie place'.

The principal landmark at the Cross was the Newton Inn (situated at its north-east corner, facing the main road, where the Texaco petrol station stands today). This was once the terminus of Porter's bus service to Giffnock station and famous for its Friday night dances. The young dancers may have learned their steps at Miss Brodie's dancing classes in Main Street. At the south-east corner of the Cross was Burn Cottage, a dairy. Both inn and cottage backed on to the fields of Townhead Farm (the neighbouring Townhead House remains) and Mearns Bowling Club, which continues to thrive, acquired some Townhead land for its green in 1920. This was feued by Arthur Gilmour after whom Arthurlie Drive and Gilmourton Crescent are named. Andersons Garage stood opposite the bowling green and diagonally opposite the inn, facing the main road south of its junction with Barrhead Road. Shops with houses above stretched along the north side of Barrhead

The bowling green was officially opened in 1921. From left to right those pictured are: James Taylor Anderson, Willie Donald, Mrs J. T. Anderson, George Slater, Fred Rodger and Andrew Russell. Townhead House, owned by Arthur Gilmour, who made available the ground for the bowling club, is in the background.

The wedding portrait of James Taylor Anderson and Jean Gilmour, daughter of Arthur Gilmour of Townhead House, c.1910.

Mearns Cross before the widening of the Ayr Road showing what became the site of the John Russell Memorial Gardens.

Road (then Newton Road) and round into Main Street (which ran parallel and to the west of the modern Ayr Road). In the 1930s three further rows of shops were built alongside Ayr Road. The row replacing the houses which had faced the Newton Inn was demolished along with the village to make way for Mearns Cross Shopping Centre, which opened in 1972 and was redeveloped as The Avenue in 1991. The other two rows of shops have survived, one of which (now largely occupied by the goldsmith Eric N. Smith) was named Central Buildings. The other, occupied mainly by fast food outlets, lies between the church and the former school.

Carrying the inscription THEIR NAME LIVETH FOR EVERMORE, the war memorial honours 39 men from the Parish of Mearns who fell in the First World War and 32 who fell in the Second World War. Originally sited in front of the former Mearns School, it was moved to its present location – the rose garden adjacent to the bowling green – in 1984, and was rededicated on 15 April that year. The rose beds were laid out at this location in 1975 by members of Mearns Horticultural Society to commemorate their late president, John Russell. He had been a lifelong member of the society, and was its president from 1945 to 1973.

The Revd MacKellar referred to fairs and a market, but over the last 100 years the only reminders of these events were the annual cattle show held until the 1950s and the flower show organised by Mearns Horticultural Society, an event which still takes place. The society was founded in 1858, and in 1969 Percy Thrower, a well-known TV gardener of the time, opened its 100th annual show. This excerpt from the centenary yearbook gives an insight into how the society was formed:

The house and garage built on the Kilmarnock (Ayr) Road in 1902 by Robert Anderson.

Robert Anderson with his wife and son John in the back garden of their house, Craigard, which was built beside the garage on the Ayr Road. The houses at Townhead Road are in the background.

No written record is available of the early years of the Society but it has been said that Mr John Russell, grandfather of the President, calling at the smiddy found some locals arguing about which of them had grown the largest cabbage. At Mr Russell's invitation they each brought their exhibits the following Saturday to his joiner's shop to have them judged. The judge's decision was hotly disputed; they agreed, however, that a competition should be organised with independent judges. This was in 1858. The first Shows were held in the Mearns Inn hall; then in the Old School [at Mearnskirk]; then in the Parish Church hall in Ayr Road, where they continued with the addition of marquees and tents overflowing into the ground next door belonging to Mr Brocklehurst, until they returned to the Main Hall of the new Mearns School [the former Mearns Primary School on Ayr Road].

   The Mearns Rose Society formed in 1897 was an offshoot of the Horticultural Society . . . Mr Neil Russell, Secretary, in the Year Book of 1901/2 reported on the great improvement in cultivation locally over the position some four or five years earlier. At the Society's Exhibition held on 20 July 1901 there were classes for Nurserymen, Gardeners and Amateurs, Confined Section, Local Amateur Section, Bouquet and Basket Section for the ladies.

Over 1,000 rose blooms were on show that day, with competitors coming from as far afield as Ireland and Dundee. Neil Russell, whose enthusiasm for cultivating roses was unbounded, named his house Rosegarth.

Andersons Garage

Between the beginning of the twentieth century and 1980 the most conspicuous landmark on the main road was Andersons Garage, which faced the war memorial and John Russell Memorial Garden. The original family firm, a coal merchants, was founded by William Anderson in Spiersbridge in 1832. William's grandson Robert, a keen cyclist, branched out on his own into the cycle business and like many others in that field developed his skills to include the internal combustion engine.

Record of one of the first cars sold by Robert Anderson in his new garage on the Kilmarnock (Ayr) Road.

Robert Cottman at his forge in Andersons Garage. In the early days of the garage motor parts often had to be fabricated on the premises.

This was the first motor ambulance in Scotland and was supplied to the Glasgow Depot of the St Andrew's Ambulance Association by Robert Anderson in August 1912. Built on a 17/25 h.p. Armstong–Whitworth chassis, it cost £438. The vehicle was subsequently written off in an accident.

There are several photographs in the company archives of accidents which Andersons attended. One wonders just how this car came to be in this position and just how Andersons managed to rescue it.

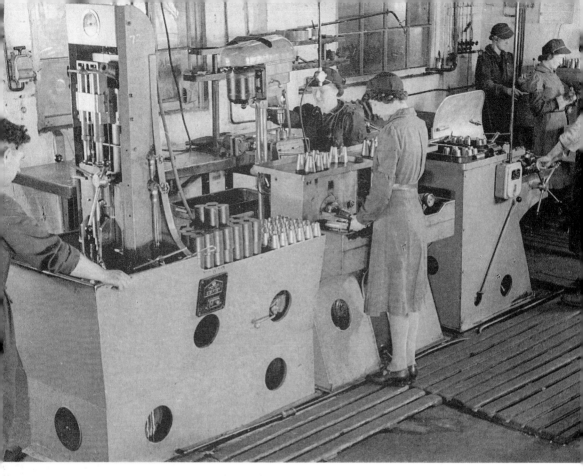

An air raid shelter in the course of construction at Andersons Garage in the early days of the Second World War. The rear of the tenement building known as Ashview Terrace in Barrhead Road is in the background.

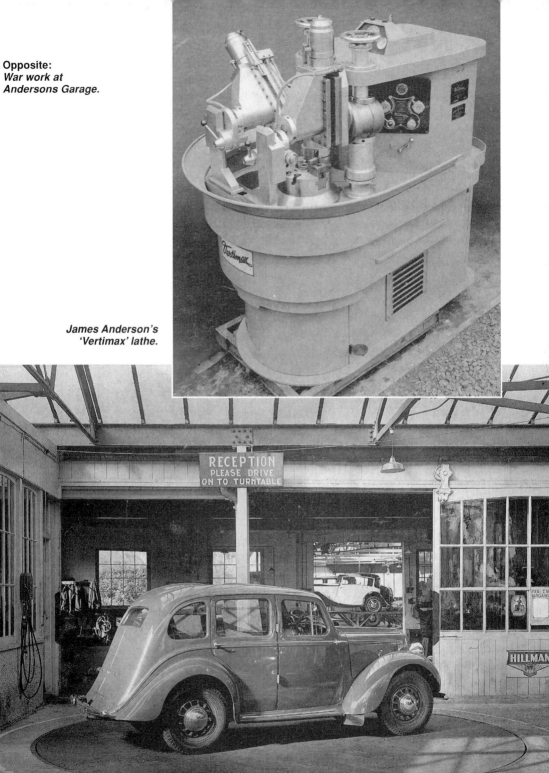

Opposite:
*War work at
Andersons Garage.*

*James Anderson's
'Vertimax' lathe.*

RECEPTION
PLEASE DRIVE
ON TO TURNTABLE

The Andersons were known for their ingenuity, an example of which was this turntable, which meant customers didn't need to reverse their vehicles on leaving the garage.

Maurice Anderson changing a wheel at a motor rally.
This car is now on display at the Museum of Transport in Glasgow.

1,700 guests were invited to Andersons Jubilee Exhibition in 1950.

In 1900 he began repairing motor vehicles, the first of which was an Albion belonging to Mr Crebar of Gorbals waterworks.

The substantial garage in Newton Mearns was established in 1902 and was followed by a branch in Giffnock in 1915. At the time motor garages were relatively few and far between and Robert Anderson's expansion was far-sighted. He rapidly acquired a reputation for thorough workmanship and built up a substantial business in what was then still a small village. In 1930 the two firms of William Anderson (coal merchants and contractors) and Robert Anderson (Andersons Garage) amalgamated as a limited company. In 1948 the coal and contracting departments were disposed of to concentrate on the motor business.

The oldest document in the company's archives is a letter dated 13 November 1899 concerning the purchase of a second-hand Beeston Humber tandem from Rennie & Prosser, cycle depot, Glasgow. By the time of their fiftieth anniversary celebrations in 1950 Andersons had become the oldest-established distributor of Humber cars – prior to that date Robert Anderson had sold Humber bicycles! The company's jubilee display centred on a new Humber Hawk flanked by two vintage Humbers – a 1903 5 h.p. two-seater and a 1905 10 h.p. four-seater, plus a 1904 Humber motorcycle – all in running order. 5,000 or more spare parts were also on show. By 1950 Humber Ltd. had become part of the Rootes Group, and among many messages of congratulation was a telegram from Sir William and Sir Reginald Rootes.

As well as selling new and used cars, Andersons had a particularly good reputation for their engineering work. During the Second World War the engineering workshop was given over to munitions manufacture for which James Anderson was subsequently awarded an MBE. He also undertook innovative work of his own, and his best known invention, patented soon after the war, was the Vertimax lathe, the manufacturing rights for which he sold to Churchill & Co. Ltd. of Birmingham in the mid-1950s (by which time he was running his own engineering firm from Thornliebank Industrial Estate). James's hobby in the inter-war years was the building and racing of sports cars (known as 'Anderson Specials'), one of which is on display in the Museum of Transport in Glasgow. His brother Maurice was awarded the Concours de Confort outright along with his co-driver Roy Hastie, the Andersons sales manager, in the Monte Carlo rallies, having competed successfully many times in the late 1940s and 1950s.

Andersons experienced problems following the takeover of Humber by Rootes, partly brought about by the withdrawal of the two-tier dealer network. In the best years of the 1950s they supplied 22 subsidiary dealers in Renfrewshire and north Ayrshire with new cars and had 130 employees on their payroll. The loss of this wholesale business led to a 60 per cent drop in sales of new cars, a loss that could not be made up in second-hand car sales. In 1980, while still in a position to meet their liabilities fully, the fourth generation directors of Andersons announced the company's closure. It was the end of an era.

Western SMT Bus Depot

During the middle years of the twentieth century a different garage became another major local employer. Western SMT drivers, conductors, conductresses, mechanics and office-workers were based at the company's Newton Mearns depot, which opened in 1932 on what is now the site of the west car park of the shopping centre.

The Mearns depot was responsible for services from Glasgow to Sheddens and Eaglesham, Clarkston and Mearnskirk, Giffnock and Newton Mearns/Mearnskirk, Barrhead

The Western SMT Bus Depot on Barrhead Road.

Bus conductresses Grace Bell (née Hunter) and Vera Frew (née Downey) pictured at the Mearnskirk terminus in the 1950s.

The forecourt of the Western SMT Garage, looking towards Ashview Terrace on Barrhead Road.

and Neilston and also for the Barrhead to Paisley route. It shared responsibility with other depots for a number of other longer routes to Ayrshire and the south-west. Special services operated to the Netherplace works, to Weir's of Cathcart, and to Hutchesons' Girls' Grammar School at Kingarth Street. Hutchie boys had to be content with the ordinary services, and walk along Cumberland Street through the Gorbals to Crown Street!

The depot was a major source of employment in the area and between the late 1940s and early 1960s serviced just under 100 buses on a daily basis. (Increasing this number to over 100 would have required enhanced salary scales for a number of key employees!) Johnny Bell was the much-respected (and sometimes feared) manager, and his standards of cleanliness and maintenance for the fleet and smartness of the staff in his control were legendary, as was his concern for the interests of the passengers. When there was a shortage of conductors he would send a bus out with another member of staff whose job was simply to ring the bell. Only properly licensed conductors could collect fares, so on these occasions passengers would get to work or school on time and travel free!

Newton Mearns residents enjoyed a remarkable service to Glasgow. There were four buses per hour on the local Newton Mearns / Mearnskirk run with the basic level on the Ayr route also four buses an hour. This meant a seven or eight minute service throughout the day from Mearns Cross to Glasgow. In addition there were many duplicates at rush hours (including lunchtime) and most of the buses operating on the Clyde Street routes picked up Mearns passengers on their way to commence or finish their duties.

By the 1960s the premises required upgrading, but extension was impossible as the local authority was planning the redevelopment of the Mearns Cross area as a suburban shopping centre. Instead, the garage relocated to a designated industrial site in Thornliebank in 1968.

Dr Fordyce

In the park alongside the bus garage was a football pitch with so steep a gradient that the crossbar of the goalposts at the Fairweather Hall end was invisible from the corner flag at the swings end. Fordyce Court, the design of which takes full advantage of the sloping site, has since been built on this part of the park and was formally opened by Dr Fordyce and his wife on 23 March 1978. The development comprises 36 sheltered flats for the elderly along with guest rooms, a communal lounge and a warden's house – all situated close to shops and public transport. Daffodils given by the Fordyces bloom every spring on the grassy banks between the flats and Capelrig Road.

Fordyce Court.

Dr and Mrs Fordyce in Crookfur Park following a ceremony to mark the doctor's retirement in 1974. Their house on the Ayr Road is in the background.

Dr Fordyce, who retired in 1974, served the village and its neighbouring country districts for 48 years, having arrived in Mearns in 1926 as assistant to Dr Mackinlay. Dr and Mrs Fordyce recalled many aspects of Mearns life prior to the 'bungalow invasion'.

We lived in Kilmarnock Road until 1964 in a two-storey house [now 194 Ayr Road] of our own design, built for £1,900 on a feu let by the Templetons of Crookfur [owners of the Glasgow carpet manufacturing business]. A single row of individual houses lined the opposite side of the road and behind these lay fields where we could hear the corncrakes on summer evenings. Our bedroom was at the front and we slept with the windows wide open. In the early morning the milk lorries were the only traffic. Mr Mitchell of the Floak Farm passed each day at 5 a.m. with his milk and if he wanted a visit he put a note through the door, telephones being few and far between in those days. Consultations were also conducted from the bedroom window and calls requested.

'Come quick, doctor, it's Mary!'

'Right, I'll be along – but you've still to pay for the last one you know.'

Occasionally unpaid bills were passed to a debt collector and surprising responses could ensue. The following came from Galston:

Dear Sir,

I got the account from the police amounting to ten shillings that you have sent me for John Young but he dozent stop here and I don't know nothing about John Young.

Yours trully John Young.

Both the grocer and the butcher's boys called daily for our order, which was duly delivered by both boys on bicycles with large baskets attached. Bowman (Barrhead Road) and Pollock (Main Street) were rival grocers: both were patients so we gave them our 'patronage' month about.

When we started married life we had a young girl from Lossiemouth trained for the previous six months by my mother. The word 'servant' had already become unacceptable and 'maid' was also losing favour; by whatever name, however, we employed one at around £3 per month all found, i.e. board, uniform, training, insurance. She usually had two half days per week.

Until 1939 the class structure was simple and direct. The big houses [Balgray, Barcapel, Todhill etc.] were at the top, followed by the farms, the village and last of all the bungalow-dwellers who lived on either side of the Kilmarnock Road.

When the Bennan [a farm south-east of Eastwood Golf Club] was being prepared as a waterworks a team of Irish labourers was enlisted. On a Saturday night they tended to find their way down to the Malletsheugh. I was called up one night to one such who after the fatigue of toiling back to the huts sat down on the stove, giving me quite a deep burn to deal with . . . some weeks later the same gentleman again required my services for, returning up the path in hard frost, he wandered on to the frozen burn and had there laid to rest.

Another Malletsheugh regular during the blackout made an almost fatal error. A caring council had painted a white line at the edge of the pavement and another in the middle of the road for the safety and convenience of patrons and buses. This character was waiting for his bus at the white line in the middle of the road, greatly surprising the driver who, though slowing, inevitably knocked him over. By the time I got there a policeman was already on the scene. 'I'm afraid he'll be dead, doctor, the driver hadn't a chance'. A voice came from under the bus saying 'No, polis, I'm no' deid'!

Dr and Mrs Mackinlay pictured in retirement.

During the war Italian prisoners occupied corrugated iron huts in the fields flanking the Stewarton Road at Patterton and after they were vacated squatters moved in. Each hut was divided to house two families. One woman had thirteen children and when the fourteenth was duly delivered she said to me as I was filling up the missive for cod liver oil, orange juice, etc., 'Don't put down Burns, doctor; it's Black now'. Mildly curious, I enquired why she'd parted from Mr Burns. 'Oh, doctor, we just felt we'd nothing in common.'

A woman in the camp was once bitten by the Co-operative horse and her husband claimed compensation. I met him later looking very prosperous to be informed, 'Mind that bite the wife got? We got fifty quid and I put it on a dog. It came in at 50–1 so I bought a key to a house – you're looking at a man of property now.'

Routine medical treatment involved bandaging, stitching and 'bottles' rather than pills. Until Jamieson's the chemist opened in the 1930s, the doctor did his own dispensing. Babies were born at home and the district nurse attended the confinements, sending for the doctor only at the critical moment. Nurse Deas, who worked with Dr Mackinlay and Dr Fordyce, is said to have had to crawl into tinkers' tents at the Humbie to deliver babies, and that after cycling or walking from the village. A. Boyd Scott wrote of the parish 'humming with stories of Dr Mackinlay's secret tenderness, his surreptitious aid and his scorn of money from the poor'. The modern Mearns Medical Centre is a continuation of the Mackinlay/Fordyce practices.

Village Names

Lost with the old village were many intriguing and picturesque names – Ashview Terrace, Botanic Gardens, Hillview, Prospect House, Hope House, Castleview Dairy, Marble Arch, Teapot Close and the Doctor's Buildings. Few have survived. Robshill Court, however, is named from Robshill Farm whose owner a century ago – Robin Craig – was much respected for his farming abilities as well as being famous for his toddy making. He was treasurer of the UF Kirk and is reported to have greeted their new minister, Revd Morton, thus: 'You'll be the new meenister ... weel, I'm the treasurer and without me you can dae neethin'. Even the 'Court' element of Robshill Court is apt, the two tennis courts of Mearns Tennis Club having lain between Robshill farm buildings and Russell's yard on the west side of Main Street. Caprera Cottage, which stood on the Ayr Road approximately opposite Newton Mearns Parish Church, got its name from somewhere rather further afield: Caprera is an island off the north coast of Sardinia!

The steep hill down from Robshill, officially designated Greenlaw Road, is traditionally the Teawell Brae. The Tea Well was situated at the foot of the brae, and a commemorative trough can be seen below the vehicular entrance to Fordyce Court near the site of the well. The story goes that the water from this well made a better cup of tea than water pumped at the Barrhead Road end of Main Street, although the advent of the bus garage ultimately caused the clear water to run brown. By this time, fortunately, running water and sewage drainage had long been supplied to the village houses, the benefactor being William Mann of Whitecraigs House. His name was fittingly commemorated by a drinking fountain which was erected at the Cross and became a popular meeting place for the village worthies to chat. The widening of the A77 and demolition of the Barrhead Road properties led to its removal, and for a time it stood forlornly beside the Fairweather Hall. It now enjoys a more prominent position at the Ayr Road entrance to The Avenue shopping centre, although sadly it has lost the ornamental ball with which it was once crowned.

Caprera Cottage.

William Mann was managing director and partner in the ship-owning company Messrs Bell Brothers & McLelland of 135 Buchanan Street, Glasgow. He died in May 1904 at the age of 50 following an operation for appendicitis. In addition to providing water and sewerage services, he is said to have purchased a public house in the Newton which he closed down in an attempt to reduce the availability of alcohol in the area.

The old village houses stood in rows or were built round 'lands'. At the Robshill end of Main Street was a warren of dwelling houses affectionately known as Teapot Close. One theory to explain the name is that these families were near enough to the Tea Well to make it worthwhile to send a child for as little as a teapotful of water. Marble Arch was the imposing name for an entry into a square courtyard with several dwellings at ground level, stairs up to an open landing with further houses, and two more attic houses above that – homes for ten or twelve families, sharing wash-houses and toilets. Teapot Close residents had to go out into Main Street and round Russell's joiners yard to their spotless but somewhat remote toilet accommodation off the lane through to the park by the tennis courts.

By the works at Netherplace were the Heigh Row and the Laigh Row of cottages; on the old Mearns Road, near the Red Lion Inn, another such row was called Thumba' Ha' (Thimble Hall) because at one time it was occupied mainly by tailors. Thumba' Ha' (which stood approximately at the entrance to Shawwood Crescent) was also known as Gateside.

All these small settlements were linked by rights of way. In the middle years of the twentieth century Jimmy McGhee used to walk each right of way every New Year's Day morning to ensure its preservation. Some still remain. One path follows the burn from Netherplace to Tofts, turns up the Teawell Brae, passes Robshill, continues down Glebe Lane and Shaw Road, reaching Shaw flats (once Shaw Farm) by a lane from Hazelwood Avenue. It continues round the flats and on to Mearns Road just below the site of Thumba' Ha'. There it meets the erstwhile route from Mearns Kirk to Kirkhill, once Kirk'ilgait ('gait' in the Scots sense of 'gateway' or 'entry') and on to Busby.

The village had the usual range of shops and small businesses – grocer, butcher, baker, draper, dairy, ironmonger, cobbler, barber – even a fortune-teller – and prior to the dry

Thumba' Ha' on the Mearns Road (looking north).

poll of 1924 three public houses: the Boat, Nanny Strang's and the Newton Inn. It was a friendly place, some happy memories of which follow:

When you paid your bill in Pollock's, you'd get a wee poke of sweeties . . . Mr Pollock always wore a long snowy white apron . . . boots for the farmers were hanging all around . . . and sand-shoes and ling fish, salted and dry, hung from the ceiling (he'd cut off bits for you) . . . and paraffin oil round at the side . . . and bundles of sticks – altogether a different smell from the coffee-grinding smell of Bowman's [who was also an expert tea blender]. (Pollock's was situated at 1 Main Street at the corner of Barrhead Road. Bowman's, which later became Cooper's, 'the pure food specialists', was at 4–6 Barrhead Road near the Cross, facing south.)

The best rolls ever came from Hay's . . . you bought them round at the bake-house at the back to enjoy the lovely smell any time from 5 o'clock in the morning . . . and on Band of Hope nights you hoped to get a fern cake or a pineapple cake as well as a bag of buns.

Another more primitive bakehouse once existed at Mearnskirk at the lower end of the row of cottages called Thumba' Ha'. The story is told that when the stone walls of the bread oven wore thin, Pat McGee the baker went over the wall into the graveyard one night, collected some big, flat stones, and built them into a new oven. His livelihood thus assured, the only snag was that his loaves bore the mirrored imprint 'Sacred to the Memory of . . . '

Johnston's had the best smells – firelighters, carbolic, waxes, oils; and after going up the wide flight of steps into the front shop you could go in and in and in . . . it was all really mysterious and exciting . . . an Aladdin's cave.

Along from Pollock's in the wee lane near the Good Templar Hall you could take your laundry and for tuppence get it all mangled . . . a whole week's wash . . . you could get a caw at the handle and for a farthing you could buy 'cheuch Jeans' (toffees that stuck your teeth together) in a poke.

Main Street, with a group of women and children standing outside Mary Osborne's 'jenny a' things' shop.

Kilmarnock Road looking south. Robert Johnston's ironmonger's shop and his two-storey house have been replaced by the Lloyd's TSB building. The Neuk Tearoom is in the right foreground.

The Miss Connells in Castle View Dairy at one time carried milk in long-handled cans to their customers every morning. Their shop was never closed, except for two hours on a Sunday morning to enable the two sisters to attend morning worship in the church nearby.

In her front room _____'s mother told fortunes . . . cards, tea leaves, palm, whatever you liked . . . she took half a crown a time which was quite dear . . . folk went all the same.

Next to McCandlish the draper was the doctor's surgery with a row of beautiful green bottles along the window.

At the end of Main Street, next to Teapot Close and Paddy Black's Mission where children came from Glasgow for holidays, was Mary Osborne's 'jenny a' things' shop . . . if you were prepared to wait she'd have everything . . . she'd say 'If y' jist gie me a meenit till I lay ma han' on it' and she would . . . cinnamon stick, licorice strap, gobstopper, sherbet dabs – choices galore for a ha'penny.

Newton Mearns library occupies ground which, along with the former Trustee Savings Bank building (now Lloyds TSB Scotland), was once the location of an excellent ironmongery business and proud owner of the area's first telephone number: Newton Mearns 1. Robert Johnston & Sons were joiners, cartwrights, blacksmiths and ironmongers who advertised 'carts, lorries and all kinds of vehicles built to order' along with 'all kinds of jobbing & blacksmith work carefully executed'.

By the 1930s the telephone numbers were approaching 3,000 and a new exchange was required. This 1936 telephone exchange building (in Ayr Road between Firwood Road and Knowes Road) carries an insignia rare in Britain – the royal crest of King Edward VIII

– although the building is now disused and in a sad state of disrepair. Next to the Ayr Road entrance to Crookfur Park and Parklands stands Croyland (previously Rysland), designed by Alexander 'Greek' Thomson and built in 1874. Adjacent to it is the 1866 building constructed as the manse of the UF Church.

At the foot of the Teawell Brae were the gasworks – opposite Greenside – run by a Mr Dorward. Before North Sea gas became the norm in the last quarter of the twentieth century, coal gas was produced at small local gasworks in most towns. Gas was extracted by heating coal in retorts; it was then channelled off for storage in gasometers before being distributed.

When I was young I spent a lot of time in the gasworks and became a great admirer of Mr Dorward. His was a 24 hours a day job, seven days a week, but he had lots of spare time and used to keep hens. He specialised in Brown and White Leghorns. The gasworks were walled in but he had a hole in the wall at ground level where he could let the hens into the field – by kind permission of my father. It is hard to believe but he used to let the brown hens out first and, after they'd spread out over the nice green grass for a few hours, he could just come to the wall, whistle, and instantly the hens would run for the hole in the wall and back to their house; whereupon he let the white ones get their turn in the green field.

One of the many attractions for me was when I was allowed to hose down the red-hot char after it had been in the retorts and then drawn out when all the gas had been extracted. It was lovely to see Mr Dorward with his heavy blue shirt open down to his waist shovelling in the new lot of coal. First shovelful to the back, and then not so far, and not so far, shovelful after shovelful till it came to the entrance.

The gable end of the shed where the fires were was part of the boundary wall. On the road side it was known as the 'Hot Wa'' and many a courting couple availed themselves of its comfort on a cold winter's night. In fact I don't think a night in winter would pass without someone using it as a place to cuddle his girlfriend. Lots of children, of course, played around the Hot Wa' as well, especially in winter when out sledging.

The directors of the gas company used to call to see how things were. They walked down the Teawell Brae to have a word with Willie Dorward and with their coats, hats, gloves, umbrellas and winged stiff collars, they were every inch retired gentlemen with impeccable manners.

There were always carts with pairs of horses and men unloading coal or taking away char and sometimes a farm-cart in for ashes for the farm roads. It was a hive of industry, all hinged on one man.

Transport in Mearns

In 1895 when the Caledonian Railway Company was planning the section of its Glasgow/Ardrossan line between Whitecraigs and Neilston, a station was proposed for Mearns – to be located at Tofts below the Teawell Brae. A branch line would deliver coal supplies to the Netherplace Works. Influenced by Sir John Stirling Maxwell, however, the company laid the line further west, replacing the proposed Mearns station with Patterton station and constructing the present viaduct which carries the line west of the waterworks to

The viaduct that was built west of the waterworks to carry the Patterton–Neilston line.

Neilston. Sir John apparently wanted to feu land at Patterton for housebuilding, similar to what he had already done in Pollokshields. The platforms at Patterton station are very long, having been designed to accommodate crowds of passengers waiting for trains to the city. As an incentive a free feu was offered – on which Walden was built – but Sir John's housing ambitions at Patterton were not realised and it wasn't until 60 years later that it became a commuter station.

The results of the railway not coming to Mearns were far-reaching. Coal had to be carted from Whitecraigs or Patterton to all the works – Tofts, Netherplace, Greenfield and the gasworks: 'it was a sight always to be seen on weekdays, magnificent horses with shining harness, hauling those heavy loads of coal up the Ayr Road'. Had there been a more convenient station these works might have expanded, Mearns might have attracted more industry, and might therefore not have become the dormitory it is today. Early transport revolved around the inn:

A family called Porter ran the inn at the turn of the [twentieth] century and it was really the hub of Mearns . . . all dances and meetings were held there . . . three horse buses met the trains at Giffnock station. There was no Whitecraigs line at that time. The Porters also had horse-driven cabs which travellers could hire to continue to Netherplace or Hazelden. Gradually the Porters lost the grip of things and the new licensee was A. Guthrie Wren. He moved to East Kilbride after the veto poll – that was sad, since he'd one very beautiful daughter, Nell.

Chapter 4

Mearns Schooldays

Mearns School was originally in the glebe of Mearns Parish Church. This schoolroom was described with some pride by the minister in 1842 as 'one of the largest and airiest of any in the west of Scotland'. In it the 103 pupils were taught Latin, geography, arithmetic, English grammar, reading and writing by Mr Jackson, a 'very able and excellent teacher', whose annual salary was £34, 4s. Government reports in 1858 and 1860 commended Mr Hunter, dominie from 1847 to 1884, for his teaching ability in Latin, Greek, mechanics, algebra and geometry, while noting that he did not profess sewing. This skill was taught to the 41 girls by 'a female in the village'.

Mr Hunter became the first head teacher at Mearns Public School on Ayr Road, the centenary of the opening of which was celebrated in 1976. The clock in the tower was a later addition, a gift from Mr Gordon of Netherplace, chairman of the school board, and first came into use on 1 May 1903. An *Evening Times* article in 1956 about the school concluded: 'The tower is a well-known landmark. Once when the clock stopped, letters and phone calls arrived from Ayr, Kilmarnock, Troon and Prestwick advising of the fault. Businessmen on their way to the city were obviously missing their time check.' Sadly the clock fell into disrepair and an attempt to restore it in the 1990s proved futile. The bell, however, was removed and cleaned and is now located in the vestibule of the new Mearns Primary School. Mr Gordon also donated a flagpole for the grounds of the Ayr Road school. On Empire Day each May, when the Union flag was hoisted, the pupils stood at the salute and listened to an address by the head. The swing park – with a maypole made from the mast of a ship – was another gift from Mr Gordon to Mearns.

Mearns Public School was built to meet the requirements of the 1872 Education Act (Scotland), which legislated for compulsory schooling for all children. Mr J. D. Hamilton of Greenbank, who became chairman of the newly formed school board, provided not only the site but also the school and teacher's house. The foundation stone was laid on 29 October 1875 and the building opened to pupils on 11 September the following year, having cost £4,575 (an official opening ceremony took place two years later on 11 October 1878). 144 children enrolled initially, but the number of pupils had increased to approximately 230 within a month.

Mr Hunter moved with his pupils from Mearnskirk and continued as head teacher until 1884. His responsibilities became more taxing than in the days of volunteers, especially since the staff never totalled more than three or four, at least one of whom would be a pupil-teacher barely older than the senior pupils. In the log book on Friday 23 September

Mearns Parish School at Mearnskirk stood on the site of the present manse.

Mearns Public School in the 1880s.

1881 he wrote: 'This has been a heartless week of business – so many blockheads to look after', an entry typical of many:

> Great difficulty experienced in teaching a number of both sexes who seem to be incapable of being taught – a most irksome and laborious task.
> A good many defaulters today, some of whom seem impossible to be taught anything – verily such a task is a wearying of the flesh.
> Great blockheadism displayed by many of the irregular attendants some of whom seem to be retrograding rather than advancing.

His daughter, Miss Marion Hunter, who died aged 91 in 1934, was also a member of staff at Mearns School. After her father's retiral she served under John Downie, who was head teacher until 1919.

The following recollections of the late Mrs Jessie Simpson (née Currie) give an insight into Mearns school life in the early twentieth century.

> It was a mile and a half to school [the Currie family lived at Netherplace] . . . we used to leave about eight o'clock in the morning . . . we had lots of company . . . so many children came from the farms . . . about a hundred of us . . . I think school finished about a quarter to four because we did not get home until half past four.
> You went in the door under the clock . . . then you went into the big hall which had four classes in it . . . there was a sliding partition in the centre of the hall and two classes were in each section . . . at the back of the school they had a room we called the back room . . . there were six classes altogether . . . there was a coal fire at each end of the big hall . . . we sat at long benches and we had just planks of wood for seats – no backs or anything fancy like that. The benches were tiered.
> All the concerts and church soirees in the village took place in the school. The partition was opened up and a platform fitted. Everybody went to the concerts. It was a great occasion.
> Mr Downie was the headmaster. He had four of a family – all very clever children – Fred, Nan, Nelson and Rhona. Nelson was killed in the First World War a few days before the end of the war. I used to go to parties at their house. I remember I went to five parties one winter, going in from school, and it was great fun. We used to talk about 'old Downie' and some people didn't like him, but of course he would be strict. I liked Mr Downie, I got on fine with him and I liked his family. They were very kind. We had a long walk to school and on a wet day if we got very wet they used to take us into the house. They had a very good maid, Annie Johnstone her name was, who dried our coats and gave us tea. Mrs Downie was very nice and took in any child who got very wet. We were in for a long time and of course we thought it was marvellous – much better than lessons.
> Mr Fraser was my teacher in Standard V. I didn't like him. He was a terror for using his strap. I used to get a dozen a day and I was afraid to tell mother at home because she thought it was for lessons and it was mostly for talking and giggling. Mr Fraser always wore a morning coat and when he bent down the coat tail with the strap in it was hanging down. One day one of the boys gently pulled it out of his pocket. At lunchtime they all went up into a field at the Cross, made a

The Clark family of Malletsheugh Farm in the 1890s.

bonfire and burnt the strap! He did everything to find out who had taken it but no one would tell.

I can't remember much about the lessons but I do know we had a lot to do. We certainly had homework. We had four sums every night and exercises, and at the weekend we always had a composition to write. My sister was very friendly with the girls at Malletsheugh Farm. Their mother used to keep a bottle of ink and a pen in a hole in the wall (outside) and all the children met there in the morning and compared their exercises and changed them.

Some of us lived too far away to go home at lunchtime. In the grocer's we could get a glass of milk for a ha'penny and a bun or roll with treacle for ha'penny or with syrup for a penny. You could be unlucky and get your syrup spread with the knife from the treacle jar and get a lot of treacle in it. That went on for years until Mrs Brodie in the public house in the Main Street started a tearoom and she made dinners for the schoolchildren. She charged a penny ha'penny for a one course meal. It was very satisfying.

Everyone went to the local school. The nearest station was Thornliebank or Giffnock. Porter's horse-drawn bus left the inn at the Cross at a quarter to nine for Giffnock station and anyone going to town for the day travelled that way. Porter also had cabs for hire. Later the older pupils could go to Glasgow schools as the stations at Whitecraigs and Patterton had opened.

Sam Drysdale was a pupil at Mearns School and served as deputy head from 1952 to 1964. In 1976 he contributed memories of his Mearns boyhood to the school's anniversary magazine.

Mearns of 60 years ago was still very much a village; separated from the city by green fields and by a fairly laborious journey, it had a character of its own. With its small satellite communities of Netherplace, Tofts, Malletsheugh, Mearnskirk and Hazelden it produced a variety of characters.

Although hard work was the rule the pace of things was slower. Traffic on the main road moved at little more than ten miles per hour. The road, deep in mud in winter and dusty in summer, restricted the speed of vehicles (many of them steam-driven) which carried milk to Glasgow from the creameries of Ayrshire.

Going uphill past the school, lorries went at a walking pace and tempted the more adventurous to catch hold and perhaps even mount the tailboard. Once past the Cross a higher speed was reached, but as the road rose towards Malletsheugh it was usually possible to dismount. An added attraction was that such vehicles carried loads such as fruit and lemonade.

The traffic was sparse, however, and going to and from school it was possible to kick a ball from one side of the main road to the other. After school football went on regularly in Barrhead Road against the door of Pollock the grocer's garage. It was here that every boy learnt the arts of football. Only occasionally was the game interrupted by the law. Playing fields were non-existent but farmers' fields provided a good pitch. This could be interrupted by the farmer asserting his rights and many a game ended when Gaffer Craig or Eck Gilmour put a knife through the ball or appropriated the jackets which formed the goalposts.

School seemed a secure settled place. We knew the rules and the penalties. Justice sometimes was three-tiered, administered by headmaster, police and parents, although not always in that order.

Presiding over our playground activities was the janitor, Frankie Corrigan, who sharpened our pencils, tended our cuts and bruises and hauled wrongdoers before the headmaster. At the intervals football held pride of place and went on constantly summer and winter except for short periods when complaints from adjoining householders forced a halt. Outside of school there was always football.

As boys we also had 'girrs' or 'girds', iron hoops made by one of the local blacksmiths. These were controlled by an iron 'cleek', a hook-like piece of iron. With these we would cover many miles round the country roads and I can still hear the bell-like ring they made as we raced along. A story of these days tells of the boy who arriving home late made the excuse 'I lost my girr so I had to walk home'. Bogies or fourwheelers were made from any wheels we could lay hands on and envious eyes were cast on any pram which looked as if it might become available.

The fields, burns and lochs were free to us and we sought frog-spawn, birds' eggs, caught baggies [minnows] or tried to swim according to the season. In fine weather the whole school would set off on foot for an outing. Pilmuir Dam was a favourite venue. The crocodile would wend its way in orderly fashion to the lochside where for some hours we could play as we pleased before being re-formed for the return journey.

In winter time half-days were fairly common as poor clothing and footwear didn't stand up to wet and cold, nor was there a school bus. A fall of snow brought out an assortment of sledges. The back of an old kitchen chair was the commonest model although there were more ambitious efforts owned by children whose fathers were joiners or blacksmiths. In default of anything else the kitchen shovel did passingly well. Our run was usually the hill in what is left of the public park. The Teawell Brae running from Main Street down to Tofts could be a veritable Cresta Run, but all too soon, just as we had it in good condition, the roadman was sent to scatter grit on it.

If there was hard frost we slid on Pilmuir Dam or Netherplace Dam, but only the favoured few had skates. When conditions were right the headmaster, the banker and other notabilities were to be found at Pilmuir, with the farmers, busy at the curling.

Of happenings at school some odd events stand out: Armistice Day 1918 when one of the fathers home on leave threw open the classroom door and marched us

Primary 2 class at Mearns Public School, 1932–3.
Back row: Margaret Hyslop, Jeanie Street, Jenny Allan, Jean Inglis, Jean Campbell, Margaret Anderson, Eleanor Cassidy
Fourth row: Gordon McKelvie, Duncan Campbell, David Gilmour, Hamilton Currie, David Manchip, Hugh McMillan, _____, Miss Findlay
Third row: Nanette McDermott, Walter Poole, Alan Auld, Matthew Raeburn, David Towns, David Gardiner, Robert Blair, Robert Smith, Jean Bain
Second row: May Black, Gladys Porter, Margaret Whiteford, Betty Traynor, Anne Black, Evelyn McMeekin, Ester McMillan, Nan McGee
Front row: Jean Scott, Alec McMillan, Frank Raeburn, Robert Trotter, Bessie Erskine

outside. We were aghast at this flouting of the rules, but out we went to join a procession led by a drummer which marched round the village. When it disbanded we all went home. We turned up at school next day fearing a reckoning to come, but to our surprise things just went on as normal. Sometime in the early 1920s we were assembled in the playground armed with pieces of smoked glass, the occasion being a total eclipse of the sun. For once on such occasions the weather was perfect and to a running commentary from the headmaster the whole process was observed.

Dr McLaren assumed office as headmaster in 1919, and in 1920 set up a higher grade department. One of his higher grade pupils was John Anderson, who later taught at Mearns, Eaglesham and Giffnock schools before his appointment as head teacher of Woodfarm High School on its opening in 1962. Here are some of his recollections of Mearns School under the regime of Dr McLaren:

> Major Smith, late of the Indian army, who gave us physical training in the playground.
> Mrs Raeburn's soup kitchen in the cookery room – a bowl of soup and a hunk of bread for a penny.
> Armistice Day when the parents came and took us all out of school.
> Morning assembly with Dr McLaren leaning over the rail at the end of the hall to see if Miss Maver had arrived to play the piano.
> The hen-house we built in the field for Dr McLaren's hens. Old ham boxes were used.
> The holiday we had when Dr McLaren's first child was born and our hope that he would have a large family.
> The first real school sports with running lanes etc., held on the ladies' hockey pitch at Crookfur.
> Hugh Leitch, strict disciplinarian and devoted teacher, later head of Eaglesham School.

The year John Anderson was Dux and left for Glasgow High School was the year another enthusiastic former Mearns pupil (1923–1932), Bill Forbes, started.

> The first person that comes to mind was the 'jannie', Grandpa Corrigan as he was known to one and all. He was a man we all respected and you could go to him with all your many complaints and find a sympathetic ear. He was the greatest pencil sharpener you ever saw; with his old tobacco knife he could give your pencil the longest and sharpest point, and his every free moment seemed to be spent doing this.
> Dr Thomas McLaren was the headmaster – what a man – strict but fair, and could he swing that belt. I should know because I was on the receiving end of it many times. He developed the habit of always looking above his head before going into his back swing, the reason being he had once broken a light fitting during a belting session. On being told of the headmaster's Ph.D. we were warned not to approach him with our physical complaints as he was not that kind of doctor.
> We had at Mearns, long before school meals came into being, a soup kitchen

where for a penny you got a huge bowl of tattie soup made in the copper boiler in the science room at the rear of the school by Grandpa Corrigan's daughter Kate. I must admit to the fact that I always attempted to head the queue and then run home for my dinner – aye, that soup was good.

Gibby Graham, the maths and science teacher, also doubled as the school football team manager. One of the highlights of the football season was when we assembled in the third year class on Friday at 12.45 to select the team for the following morning.

We were proud of Mearns School and it was during the period when I was there that the school badge was designed as it is now – Mearns Castle.

Dr McLaren was succeeded by Mr Thom, who was most keen on the school choir. His energies and enthusiasm were rewarded when at Greenock town hall the choir won the Alston Trophy. My mother (Jeannie Waterhouse) was a pupil of Mearns and she instilled in us the fondness of Mearns which she held so dearly.

With the opening of Eastwood Senior Secondary School in 1937 (now Williamwood High School), pupils on higher grade courses no longer had to travel to Shawlands Academy. Junior secondary education, however, continued in Mearns School until Woodfarm opened in 1962.

Under Mr Thom life at school continued smoothly. 1939, however, included the following entries in the official log:

2 & 3 February: School closed to allow teachers to take part in the survey under government evacuation scheme.
4 May: Architect examined building with a view to arranging for protection against air raids.
11 September: School reopened after being delayed for one week owing to outbreak of war.

The primary schools which continue to serve Mearns children are Kirkhill (opened 1960), Crookfur (1973), St Cadoc's (1976) and Mearns Primary School which was officially opened by Jack McConnell, First Minister of Scotland, on 17 June 2002. These schools presently have a roll of over 2,000. An exciting development in recent years has been the inclusion of nursery education within primary schools and the new Mearns Primary School has such provision. It was built under the PFI (Private Finance Initiative) scheme, and is the largest primary school in East Renfrewshire, known locally as the 'Mearns Monster'. Secondary school education is provided at Eastwood High, Mearns Castle High and St Ninian's High Schools. A private school, Belmont House, offers pre-school, primary and secondary education and has just under 350 pupils on the school roll. Many people from outwith the area send their children to Mearns schools in recognition of their high academic standards. Others, attracted by the quality of education available, choose to move to Newton Mearns.

Following the opening of the new Mearns Primary School the old school on Ayr Road was closed, and at the time of writing East Renfrewshire Council plans to sell it to provide more parking space for The Avenue shopping centre. The developers would be allowed to demolish the stone building, which is a well-known landmark and regarded as part of the area's heritage. There has been much local opposition to the proposals.

Chapter 5

Wartime Comings and Goings

Evacuees from Glasgow arrived in Newton Mearns in September 1939, and these abruptly changed days were recalled in 1976 by Miss E. A. Calder for Mearns School's anniversary magazine. Miss Calder joined the staff in January 1938 and retired in June 1971, thus perhaps seeing more changes than any other member of staff. The following paragraphs are summarised from her memories.

> The mustering point for the evacuees was the school and on the sunny September day when they arrived small groups from St Alphonsus' in London Road were dotted all over the playground. There were double the number that had been expected as those intended for Busby School arrived in Newton Mearns too. The famous 'Panic Bus' brought last minute evacuees such as expectant mothers.
>
> It's a stark comment on the social conditions in Glasgow's east end at the time that most of the evacuees had lice, and no sooner had they been allotted to their billets than Mearns fathers were dashing out for Dettol as the parasites spread through their households.
>
> Those that couldn't be accommodated with families on the first night were billeted in the infant rooms of the school on straw palliasses and a field kitchen was set up, manned by Miss Buchanan and Miss Mackenzie. Come morning the palliasses were crawling with lice and had to be burned.
>
> On the third day classes were due to begin and there were over 80 children in the infant room – sitting at desks, on the floor and on window sills. Miss Ritchie and her staff were trying to cope when three female HMIs [school inspectors] arrived complete with khaki knitting to interview Miss Ritchie about what she was doing. They were told to GET OUT!

About 100 children who had previously attended Glasgow schools enrolled at Mearns on the first day of the new school year, and in subsequent sessions the roll fluctuated month by month by hundreds, an organisational nightmare for Mr Thom and his staff. As his wife later recalled:

> The change was cataclysmic. From Glasgow came youngsters who had scarcely, if ever, seen green fields or heard the songs of birds and smelt the fragrance of flowers. All these children had to be housed and educated in a wee quiet village.

The school was overwhelmed. Every available hall in the district was put to use: even the ground floor of the schoolhouse was utilised.

The countryside proved no substitute for fish suppers and the cinema, however. 'Nae fish 'n chips . . . nae picturs . . . ahm gaun hame' was the cry in many a home, especially from the young mothers who had been evacuated with their babies and younger children. At the beginning of the 1939–40 session the school roll increased from 471 to 776 due to the presence of the evacuees, but many soon returned to their home areas and the number of extra pupils became slightly more manageable.

During wartime special fund-raising events were regularly held and Mearns School contributed to these. In Warships Week, April 1942, £840 was raised and almost £1,500 was collected during May 1943's Wings for Victory drive. Alongside such special events and an occasional air raid alert, normal schoolwork continued from day to day. Each autumn the older boys did potato lifting on the local farms.

Mearns escaped direct enemy action (although some bombs fell in the area) and the nearest targets lay along the River Clyde more than seven miles away. In 1941 civilian deaths in Britain from enemy bombing approached 20,000, over 1,000 of these being the result of the blitz on Clydebank on 13/14 March. The previous year had also been bad for Britain with 24,000 killed, half of them in London.

In such circumstances it is not surprising that many families concerned about the safety of their children took advantage of the evacuation liners which sailed to Canada and the United States. In the first week of August 1940, for instance, three liners of child refugees reached Canada and two berthed in New York. At the end of that same month the Dutch liner *Volendam* left the Clyde with over 300 evacuee children on board, including two brothers from 76 Larchfield Avenue. The younger boy withstood an amazing ordeal, which almost a year later was featured in *The Bulletin* of Thursday 15 May 1941. Robert Wilson was asleep in his cabin when a torpedo struck the *Volendam*, but managed to sleep through the confusion, waking to discover his cabin empty and the ship seemingly deserted. The following morning he saw a destroyer lying alongside. On shouting across to it for assistance, he attracted the attention of a member of the *Volendam*'s skeleton crew (previously he had thought the ship was deserted). *Volendam* was towed to a west of Scotland port and Robert was reunited with his parents.

Rudolf Hess – Mysterious Stranger

Perhaps the most famous uninvited guest to arrive in Britain last century was Rudolf Hess, who parachuted onto farmland between Mearns and Eaglesham as darkness fell on the evening of Saturday 10 May 1941. His Messerschmidt 110 evaded two Hurricanes sent up by Coastal Command in Northumberland and a Defiant from RAF Prestwick before its solitary occupant rolled his aircraft over, ejected, and left it to crash. Ploughman David McLean found the German pilot entangled in his parachute and from his cottage Home Guardsmen Robert Gibson and Jack Paterson took 'Oberleutnant Alfred Horn' into custody. He was initially taken to the village hall at Busby before being held in Giffnock police station and then transferred to Maryhill barracks.

This first capture of an enemy officer of obvious high rank aroused great local excitement – even before the news of his real identity was disclosed the following week. The Russell family at Newton House heard the news from their neighbour Mr Thom, headmaster at

These soldiers, pictured outside one of the Emergency Medical Service wards at Mearnskirk Hospital, must have experienced amazement if not incredulity when it became known that Rudolf Hess, the Deputy Fuehrer of Germany, had parachuted into a field about a mile away on the evening of 10 May 1941. This photograph shows part of his Messerschmidt nailed to the wooden hut.

Mearns School and Home Guardsman, as the late Miss Isa Russell recalled:

> We heard the plane, of course, but only Elizabeth saw it. She was seeing off Willie McLaren (later her husband) and they watched it from the front garden. That was why she'd been out so long – so she claimed!
>
> Then on the Sunday afternoon, over our garden wall from the schoolhouse garden climbed Mr Thom in his Home Guard uniform, gun and all – he was going on duty – to tell us that the previous evening late a German plane had crash-landed at the Floors and a senior German officer been picked up by the duty Home Guards. On being asked why such an officer was likely to have flown so far from his homeland, Mr Thom's explanation was crisp and unforgettable. 'The rats always leave the sinking ship.'

The low-flying plane had been widely noticed in the stillness of that summer evening. Another ear-witness was the late Mrs Jean Fordyce:

> We remember the night well. Friends had come in and although it was still light we had already put up the blackout as it took so long. We heard the thrum of a

low-flying aircraft and had we looked out we would also have seen it. Sadly we did not.

However next day the doctor was over at Floors Farm. He said to Mrs Baird, 'I hear you had a German officer drop in on you last night'. She said, 'Yes, I was just going up to bed at the time and I saw a white thing on the hedge. I thought I'd left my bleaching out and went back down as the men came in and said, 'It's a German in a white uniform.' 'Oh,' I said, 'is that it?' and went back to bed.'

The British government maintained a very low profile on so mystifying an event. Not until 11.20 p.m. on Monday 12 May was official word issued that Hess was in British hands. The communique from 10 Downing Street read:

Rudolf Hess, Deputy Fuehrer of Germany and Party Leader of the National Socialist Party, has landed in Scotland under the following circumstances:

On the night of last Saturday an Me 110 was reported by our patrols to have crossed the coast of Scotland and to be flying in the direction of Glasgow. Since an Me 110 would not have the fuel to return to Germany, this report was at first disbelieved.

Later on an Me 110 crashed near Glasgow with its guns unloaded. Shortly afterwards a German officer who had baled out was found with his parachute in the neighbourhood suffering from a broken ankle. He was taken to a hospital in Glasgow where he at first gave his name as Horn, but later he declared he was Rudolf Hess.

He brought with him various photographs of himself at different ages, apparently in order to establish his identity. These were deemed to be photographs of Hess by several people who knew him personally. Accordingly, an officer of the Foreign Office, who was closely acquainted with Hess before the War, has been sent up by aeroplane to see him in hospital.

Among the questions Hess put to the first Scots he met was one concerning the proximity of their farm cottage to Dungavel, the Duke of Hamilton's residence. It transpired that Hess's plan had been to make contact with the Duke of Hamilton (who he had previously met at the 1936 Olympic games in Berlin) and recruit the Duke as a confidante with the intention of providing information about the Nazi war machine to the British and negotiating peace.

Prior to the revelations from the British government, reports from Germany announced that Hess, apparently suffering from poor mental health, had made a solo flight and was thought to have died in a crash. He had in fact landed 940 miles north-west of Augsburg and within a few miles of his destination – a remarkable feat from a technical and navigational point of view.

Having been confined at Buchanan Castle, Drymen, Hess was taken secretly to the Tower of London before being imprisoned elsewhere in Britain until 6 October 1945. The outcome of his trial at Nuremberg as a war criminal was the life imprisonment sentence which he served in Spandau prison, West Berlin, under rotating Soviet, French, British and American military guard, until his death in August 1987. The anonymous arrival of such an important ally of Hitler's in Britain was remarkable enough in its own right – the fact that he landed just outside Mearns was even more astonishing.

Chapter 6

Open Air Hospital at Southfield

The afternoon of Sunday 3 July 1949 found the Kirkintilloch Junior Choir and Springburn Military Band in the grounds of Mearnskirk Hospital. The occasion was the unveiling of a bronze statue of Peter Pan – a memorial to the hospital's first medical superintendent, Dr John A. Wilson OBE.

Following service in the First World War and research work in bacteriology, Dr Wilson joined the tuberculosis service of Glasgow Corporation in the 1920s. He worked in the East End and at Ruchill Hospital until 1929, when he was appointed superintendent of Mearnskirk Hospital for Children, then still under construction. At the same time he was appointed senior lecturer in clinical tuberculosis at Glasgow University, holding both posts with distinction until his death in July 1946.

Dr Wilson had always been keenly interested in enhancing the beauty of the hospital's extensive grounds, and during the 1930s had arranged for several small statues of child figures – designed to appeal to children – to be installed. These were made of cement, however, and were vulnerable to the elements in so exposed a position as Mearnskirk. In the light of this he hoped to erect a more permanent bronze statue and settled on the choice of Peter Pan (possibly partly because the father-in-law of his colleague Dr Dale had been one of J. M. Barrie's childhood friends in Kirriemuir). Although Dr Wilson never lived to see the statue unveiled, Alfred Ellsworth promised him on his deathbed that it would become a reality. Mr Ellsworth was a close friend of Dr Wilson's and a generous benefactor to the children both in Mearnskirk and in deprived areas of the city. He was awarded an MBE for his philanthropy.

This promise led to a fund being launched and its fulfilment came with the unveiling ceremony in the summer of 1949. A souvenir brochure marked the occasion, in which Alex Proudfoot RSA, the sculptor, described his commission and the genesis of the bronze statue.

The Corporation of Glasgow had bought Southfield House and its policies, along with the farms of Hazelden Head, Westfield, Eastfield and Langrig, in 1913. Their original intention had been to convert the mansion into a country home for pre-tuberculous children, but building operations were delayed by the First World War, during which the house deteriorated to such an extent that it had to be demolished. The estate policies of Southfield House had also fallen into decline during changes of tenancy around the start of the twentieth century, but happily the opening of the hospital led to their restoration. Pavilions were planned to treat 160 adults and 300 children suffering from TB. The name of the institution was initially to be Southfield Sanatorium, but this was rejected because of the

Mearnskirk Hospital's brick chimney was once a well-known landmark.

Opposite:
Heliotherapy (exposure to sunlight) was part of the treatment for those suffering from tuberculosis, as was rest and good food.

Mr Shepherd, groundsman. The grounds of the hospital were beautifully landscaped.

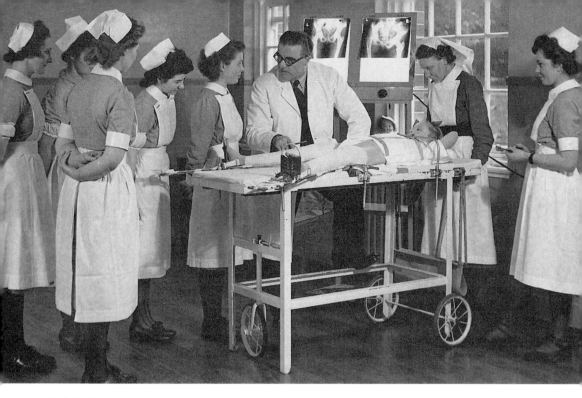

Dr Dale, the second medical superintendent of the hospital, teaching in the Nurses' School.

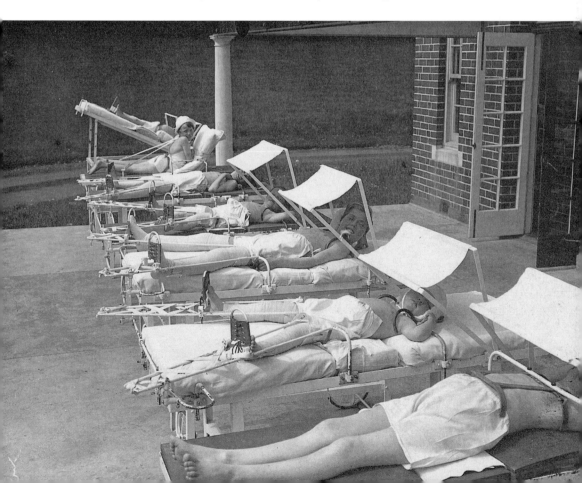

Miss Taylor and some young patients in the 'underwater exercise pool'. Physiotherapy including hydrotherapy played an important role in the treatment of those who had received corrective orthopaedic surgery.

Patients receiving lessons from Miss Fergus, May 1955. Children often spent many months at Mearnskirk and provision was made for their education.

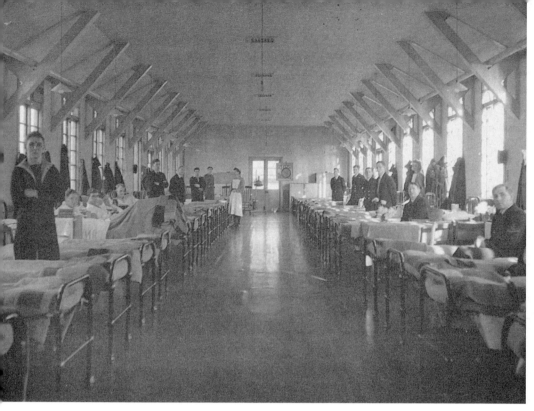

Naval personnel at Mearnskirk.

Nurses relaxing off-duty.

The film star Dorothy Lamour
visits Mearnskirk hospital.

Alfred Ellsworth pictured with
two young Glaswegians.

Two little girls admire a cement statue of Wendy of Peter Pan fame, one of a number of small statues which Dr John Wilson OBE, the first medical superintendent, erected in the grounds of the hospital.

The Peter Pan statue was unveiled in July 1949 in memory of Dr Wilson. It has since been relocated outside Mearnskirk House, but in a somewhat attenuated form without the bronze panels which are believed to have been stolen.

Patients playing in the sunshine. Conditions at Mearnskirk must have been very different from those in the city hospitals.

The cardio-thoracic operating theatre at Mearnskirk in the early 1970s.

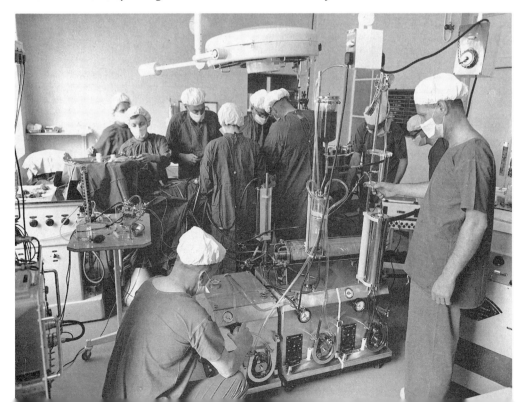

Edinburgh hospital of the same name. The name Mearnskirk was adopted in deference to the proximity of Mearns Parish Kirk, and having dropped plans for adult beds the full name became Mearnskirk Hospital for Children.

Sir Alexander Macgregor, Medical Officer of Health for the City of Glasgow from 1925 to 1946, recounts in his memoirs that the 'hospital narrowly escaped being postponed indefinitely under the post [World War I] national economy measures'. A 'cart load of bricks' was delivered to the site at the suggestion of a senior secretary of the Scottish Board of Health so that he could report to the Treasury that building work was underway and the project could not be stopped.

Construction began in 1921 and Dr Wilson became superintendent in 1929. The first patients were received in 1930 and Dr Alexander Dale, then assistant medical superintendent, described the opening days thus:

> The first patients arrived as arranged on 9 May and were children suffering from surgical tuberculosis, transferred from Robroyston Hospital where they had been accommodated pending the opening of Mearnskirk. The first patient was George McEwan, aged 6 years, who stepped from the ambulance proudly carrying a large box of cigarettes for Dr Wilson from the staff at Robroyston.
>
> The hospital was officially opened by HRH the Duchess of York [the late Queen Mother] on 12 October 1932. To mark the occasion Her Royal Highness planted a royal oak on the main avenue and this tree has grown and flourished with the development of the hospital.

Pre-Second World War Mearnskirk with its broad verandahs was primarily a children's orthopaedic hospital, treating children with TB of the spine, hip and other bones and joints. As treatment was often prolonged, the educational, recreational and spiritual needs of the young patients had also to be addressed. Teachers were employed and hosts of friends visited, ran Scouts, Guides, Sunday schools, and so on. Dr Wilson's recognition of the importance of these activities for his patients' well-being was not outweighed by his clinical interests in pulmonary TB or his bacteriological research work, and the staff were similarly minded.

An amazing number of celebrities came to the hospital through the good offices of Alfred Ellsworth MBE, including Roy Rogers, Danny Kaye, Terry Thomas, Eddie Calvert, Ann Shelton, Sir Harry Lauder, Jimmy Logan and Dorothy Lamour. Other less well-known visitors also made a significant contribution to improving the lives of the patients. An article from the *Glasgow Herald* of January 1980 reported the death of 'Mrs Thursday', an 83 year old lady who had spent over 30 years visiting the hospital (on Thursdays!), only ceasing to do so when she lost her sight.

At the outbreak of the Second World War the Emergency Medical Service took over most of Mearnskirk's pavilions after 287 child patients had been evacuated to Millport. A hutted annexe of fifteen wards (each with accommodation for 40 patients) was built to add 600 beds and was ready for occupation by April 1940. The EMS provided treatment for 30,799 naval personnel and 1,810 civilian casualties over the next six years.

Following the release of the hospital from emergency service on 31 August 1946, and as a direct result of innovations in the surgical treatment of pulmonary TB, Pavilion 7 was converted into a fully equipped theatre unit capable of dealing with all aspects of thoracic surgery. The first patients were admitted in November 1946. Mr Bruce Dick of Hairmyres

Hospital was visiting consultant surgeon and Mr R. S. Barclay was in charge of the day-to-day running of the unit. Under their leadership Mearnskirk became recognised as a leading centre for thoracic surgery, renowned both in Britain and abroad.

In 1948, with the inception of the National Health Service, Mearnskirk transferred from the control of the Corporation of Glasgow to the Western Regional Hospital Board and the board of management for the Glasgow Victoria Hospitals. An ear, nose and throat department was established the same year and was active until 1986.

Meanwhile the reputation of the thoracic unit continued to grow, and its importance was recognised when in 1955 the Society of Thoracic Surgeons of Great Britain and Ireland held its annual meeting at Mearnskirk. Initially the unit mainly treated cases of pulmonary tuberculosis, but as new drug therapies were developed most TB patients recovered from their illness without recourse to major chest surgery. This meant that from the early 1950s more and more closed-heart surgery was performed, for instance mitral valvotomies (to open the mitral valve after it has narrowed as a result of rheumatic fever). By the late 1950s it became possible to perform open-heart surgery when the technique of hypothermia was introduced. By lowering body temperatures from 37° C to 30° C the brain could withstand a lack of oxygen for up to seven minutes, during which time uncomplicated 'holes in the heart' such as atrial septal defects could be repaired.

The introduction of the heart/lung machine in the early 1960s allowed operating times to be significantly extended so that more complicated open-heart surgery could be performed. By this time the unit was recognised as the principal cardio-thoracic referral centre for the south-west of Scotland. In 1971 state-of-the-art twin theatres were installed in the unit and heart valve replacements and coronary artery bypass graftings were performed. As part of a reorganisation of specialist care in Glasgow hospitals and to the regret of the team, the cardio-thoracic unit was closed in 1981.

From 1959 Mearnskirk was officially designated a general hospital, and different treatments and services were offered as medical and political priorities changed. Latterly the orthopaedic unit became a centre for the assessment and treatment of cerebral palsy but closed following the retirement of Mr Kenneth Guest in 1977. In the years before its closure most of Mearnskirk's patients were again long-stay as the hospital played a major role in geriatric care for the south side of Glasgow.

In the early 1990s Greater Glasgow Health Board sold the hospital grounds and buildings to a consortium of developers comprising John Dickie Homes, Bryant Homes and Stewart Milne Homes, which built a total of 261 houses and 107 flats in the prestigious Mearnskirk Hospital development. There was much local dismay when it was reported in *The Glasgow South and Eastwood Extra* in May 1996 that the oak tree planted by the Queen Mother on 12 October 1932 to mark the official opening of the hospital had been felled by the consortium. It was claimed that the felling of the tree was an error, but despite this a fine of £15,000 was imposed at the Sheriff Court for removing a protected tree. John Dickie Homes won a Civic Trust award in 1999 for the development of the former Nurses' Home, now named Southwood Place.

A long-term continuing care hospital, Mearnskirk House, was opened on the hospital site in 1998, and is owned by Walker Timber Products Ltd. It consists of two wards, Lanrig and Millbrae, each with 32 single and two double rooms. Services are provided by Sodexho, and the hospital is staffed by NHS personnel from the South Glasgow University Hospitals Trust. A children's nursery, Hazeldene House, run by East Renfrewshire Council, operates in what was the hospital's administrative building.

Chapter 7

Big Houses . . . No More

The tree-lined avenue leading into the grounds of the former Mearnskirk Hospital is a reminder of the many fine estates of earlier times. In *Old Days and Ways in Newton Mearns*, A. Boyd Scott states that significant changes in the proprietorship of land occurred in the county between 1772 and 1832, when nearly a third of it changed hands. A number of new big houses appeared when affluent merchants and others, such as the Barclays at Capelrig and the Hutchisons at Southfield, came to the area. 47 heritors were listed in the *New Statistical Account* of 1842, along with the valuation of their properties. They ranged from Mr Harvie of Greenlaw at £8 to the Polloks of Upper Pollok at £1,409, 5s., 10d. However, while the Revd MacKellar expressed admiration for the 'excellent modern mansions' of his country parish, Christopher North was more cynical, commenting on 'modern villas, or boxes, inhabited by persons imagining themselves gentlemen, and, for anything we know to the contrary, not wholly deceived in that belief'.

Pollok

Although most of these houses survived into the twentieth century, few remain nowadays in anything like their original form. Gone, for example, is the property which headed Mr MacKellar's valuation list, Pollok Castle. Several houses have graced the estate and the last one (dating from 1886) was built in the Scots baronial style by the Fergusson Polloks. This splendid mansion was used by the military during the Second World War (ammunition was stored in the grounds), but gradually fell into disrepair and was demolished after the death of Miss Fergusson Pollok in 1954. The former lodge houses and stables have been converted into private houses. New plans for the estate came to public notice when it was announced in *The Herald* in November 2001 that a luxury housebuilder, Manor Kingdom, planned to build a 'magnificent one-off mansion on the site of the former Pollok Castle'. This is now nearing completion.

Crookfur

At the heart of present-day Newton Mearns lies Crookfur Estate – now the site of cottage homes belonging to the Retail Trust. The trust's patron is Her Majesty the Queen, who visited the homes and planted a tree in the grounds on 3 July 1979. Until the 1950s Crookfur was the home of the Templetons, a branch of the carpet manufacturing family whose

The Renaissance-style Pollok Castle which dated from 1694 and was destroyed by fire in 1882.

Crookfur House, in the grounds of which the Crookfur Cottage Homes were built.

The Crookfur Cottage Homes.

former factory, situated on the edge of Glasgow Green, was built in the style of the Doge's Palace and is still a prominent landmark today. A picture of Crookfur's grounds and glasshouses was provided for the Horticultural Society's centenary yearbook by Alan MacCallum, gardener to the Templeton family between the wars:

> Crookfur House ... was a charming old mansion clad in front with ivy, the windows looked out on to a pleasant lawn and the planted grounds around, studded with hardy trees among which were fine groups of rhododendron. Shady walks pursued a wandering course around the grounds and were enjoyable retreats even for the gardeners in hot summer days. Countless snowdrops and daffodils were naturalised in clusters and drifts and were a delight in the grass around the bare feet of the trees in spring.
>
> The flower garden, which was within the main walled garden, was within easy reach of the front door. The walled garden was probably an acre in extent; a gravel path edged with boxwood ran round the garden with ribbon borders up to the walls, on which apples and plums were trained. There were also two small orchards.
>
> Grass walks intersected the rose and flower beds and were mown with an eighteen inch tracing mower, myself pulling in front and another man pushing at the back. The main lawn was cut with a 36 inch horse-drawn mower which must have weighed fully three hundredweight [about 150 kg]. The motive power, a fresh hunter, had to be tethered to a stake in the field and trotted around for a couple of hours before being yoked. Grass mowing day was an exciting if exhausting business with this animal. I was much relieved when the decision was taken to hire a staid, canny Clydesdale for this job. In a few years, however, we had a petrol-driven machine and could mow the lawns when convenient for us rather than the hiring contractor.
>
> The glass consisted of a peach house, a vinery, a fig house, and a fernery. Two greenhouses stood apart from the main range. The vines grown here were Black

Hamburg, a well-flavoured variety. Figs were of easy culture and two crops could be taken, one from the shoots of the previous year's growth and those of the current year for the second crop. The variety grown was Brown Turkey.

The field where the 'fresh hunter' had to be trotted before Mr MacCallum could yoke him to the mowing machine lies alongside Ayr Road and nowadays is Crookfur Park. Before the Second World War it was leased for grazing to the Harvies of Shieldhill and Langbank Farms. Their cows had to be chased out of the way whenever 'young Mr Templeton' wanted to land his light aeroplane. The story is told that shortly before his marriage he took the staff for a short flight around the district – one at a time – finishing with the housemaids and last of all the cook. The plane was started by a flick of the propellor and so, having installed the cook, this the son of the house proceeded to do – forgetting he had left the throttle open. Knocking him aside, off went the cook on her first and last solo flight, the plane careering across the field before coming to rest in a hedge. All parties escaped unscathed apart from some decidedly frayed nerves.

In the 1950s Crookfur was sold and functioned briefly as a country house hotel, although in the course of changing hands again it was so damaged by fire that it had to be demolished. Drapers' trade benevolent organisations acquired the estate in 1960 and seven years later the present cottage homes were opened by Lady Fraser of Allander. Designed by the architect Sir Basil Spence, whose best-known commission is Coventry Cathedral, the original complex consisted of 50 cottages and self-contained flats. One of the original criteria for potential residents was that they should have been employed for at least 25 years in the drapery trade; the present requirement is that they must have worked in the retail trade for a minimum of ten years.

Today the accommodation consists of 52 cottages and 53 flats for independent residents. In June 2000 an award-winning extension to the care home was opened, with 40 beds now available for those requiring residential care. This is in addition to thirteen recently completed studio flats designed to promote independent living for those who would otherwise require residential care. Despite these additions and extensions, gardens and woodlands have been skilfully retained so that the complex still has the feel of a country estate. Since its inception it has provided a pleasant, safe and comfortable environment for the elderly, and it is to be hoped that it will do so for many years to come.

Broom

The neighbouring mansion house and estate of the Broom did not remain a family home as long as Crookfur. The estate name survives as a district of Mearns, but the mansion house (built in 1840 and described as 'a very elegant modern mansion') has long had a new name and function, as Belmont House School. This area of Mearns has undergone immense change since the inter-war years when Belmont's founder bought the mansion house and two acres of garden, along with a three acre plot for playing fields a short distance away. Broom House could then be approached from two lodge houses on the Kilmarnock (Ayr) Road. Its main driveway is now Sandringham Avenue, and the stable buildings at the former side entry have been redesigned as Lochbroom Court luxury flats.

In September 1929 G. A. Montague Dale and his wife Beryl opened a preparatory school for boys in Greenhill Avenue near Eastwood Toll. Its name – Belmont – was an amalgam of their first names. The school grew quickly from its initial roll of 22 and new accommodation was required; hence the Broom mansion house was acquired. A wooden assembly hall from the Giffnock site was re-erected north of the Victorian mansion along with several classrooms, and both school and playing fields were surrounded by a high wooden fence. Mactaggart & Mickel had bought the estate land surrounding the school and began to build houses there before the Second World War.

For Belmont's golden jubilee in 1979 former pupil Neil Gow, now a QC, wrote a short history recalling the school and its surroundings in the thirties and during the war. Some extracts from his recollections are quoted here:

Nearly all the pupils in the thirties came from well-to-do families, although perhaps we did not realise it at the time. Most boys attended school from private residences on the south side of Glasgow, particularly Whitecraigs, the Broom Estate as it expanded, Giffnock, Newton Mearns, Clarkston and also Pollokshields. Most houses in those districts which were built in the twenties and thirties had a maid's room or servants' quarters attached to the kitchen premises. Some of them had double garages with a flat above for the chauffeur or gardener. When one visited the home of a school friend there was invariably at least a housemaid, and sometimes one or more other domestic servants.

In the thirties, quite a number of boys arrived at Belmont in limousines driven by liveried chauffeurs. Many boys also had nannies, who arrived at school wearing their long grey coats, black hats and gloves in order to collect their precious charges.

In the lower forms the school fee was eight guineas per term, rising to twelve guineas in the higher forms [a guinea was equal to 21 shillings]. Extras were offered at two guineas per term including pianoforte, elocution, dancing and

Belmont School photographed in the early 1930s when it was located in Greenhill Avenue.

boxing. Each Friday afternoon Mr Carswell would come out from his gymnasium in Glasgow to teach us the rudiments of the noble art. Actual fighting between boys was not permitted until the very end of the lesson, when we were allowed one 60-second round with a friend of equal size and weight, thus ensuring the rapid and immediate exhaustion of all the participants.

Kirkhill

Over the hill from Belmont, and lying east of the Church of Broom and Kirkhill Primary School in Broom Road East, is Kirkhill House. Built in 1873, it is presently the headquarters of C. W. Cameron Ltd. In 1963 it became the Thomson Television College to which students from different parts of the world came to learn about television production. Lord Thomson of Fleet visited the college in 1973 and planted a Canadian maple tree at the entrance to mark the house's centenary.

Balgray, Capelrig and Greenbank

Three Georgian mansion houses survive: Balgray, Capelrig and Greenbank. Only Balgray, the smallest, remains as a family home (another 'big hoose', Todhill, albeit not Georgian, is also a family home). Capelrig House belongs to East Renfrewshire Council and Greenbank to the National Trust for Scotland.

Greenbank Estate dates from the 1760s when Glasgow merchant Robert F. Allason had the house built in policies extending to 250 acres. It has had many owners, the last of whom, Mr and Mrs William Blyth, presented the property to the National Trust for Scotland in 1976. In accordance with the wishes of the donors, a gardening advice centre was set up where amateur gardeners may seek expert advice from the three NTS gardeners who tend the garden. Every February the woodlands are carpeted with single and double snowdrops and later in the spring many varieties of narcissus bloom. Within the walled garden 3,500 varieties of shrubs and hardy flowers are cultivated, demonstrating clearly which plants best tolerate West of Scotland conditions at 500 feet above sea level. Greenbank

Balgray House, one of three Georgian houses still in existence in the area.

Garden is one of five gardens in the United Kingdom where trials are conducted for the Consumers Association.

Greenbank is known for its daffodil collection which now numbers 340 different varieties. Sadly there is no record of the original plantings in the 1920s and 30s so some are unnamed. On Daffodil Day (an annual event) in 2003, 250 different named forms were on display in the house. In the south-east portion of the garden, where the tennis courts used to lie, is a greenhouse and garden designed for disabled visitors. The greenhouse has a wide door for easy access and the garden has raised beds and pool features. A feature of note is the Sensory Garden, which includes plants known for their taste, touch, smell, sound and movement.

About four years after Greenbank House was built, another fine country mansion was constructed at Capelrig for a member of the 'Glasgow gentry'. 200 years later, when the estate was chosen as the site for the new Eastwood School, Capelrig House was threatened with demolition. A campaign to save it led to interest from the Georgian Society. The Secretary of State for Scotland also became interested and when it became apparent that planning permission would be granted only if the house was retained, the county council offered Capelrig House to the district council. After £40,000 had been spent by the latter to arrest almost 40 years of neglect, Capelrig House became a community centre, but is now used as office space for East Renfrewshire Council. Birney Boyd, an American pupil, offered the readers of the 1969 *Eastwood Magazine* the fruits of his researches into the Capelrig site, some of which are reproduced here:

The name 'Capelrig', which occurs in a twelfth century document, is thought to be derived from 'Chapel-Ridge', suggesting that there may at one time have been a church situated on the estate. In 1300 Herbert de-Maxwell endowed a chapel in Mearns, perhaps at Capelrig, but today there remains no evidence of this.

The two crosses on the [school] badge are a reminder that the Knights Templar once owned the lands of Capelrig. They used a single red cross on a white background as their emblem; the colours have been reversed on the Eastwood badge. The Knights Templar were founded in 1119 and introduced into Scotland by David I (1124-53). They took vows of poverty (riding two on one horse), chastity and obedience, and were established to care for Christian pilgrims visiting the Holy Land, and to defend the Temple and Holy Sepulchre in Jerusalem from the Saracens. They were half-soldiers, half-monks and eventually gained land in every parish in Scotland.

The Capelrig Cross, an ancient Celtic monument, would have been considered old by the Templars when they first settled on the estate. The oldest relic of Christianity in the parish, it dates from around AD 900 and originally stood in a field north-east of Capelrig House. Only the shaft remains, which was removed to Kelvingrove Art Gallery in 1926.

There is an ancient legend connected with this cross. Its original site was said to be one of the points of an isosceles triangle, the second point of which was located in the middle of Ryat Linn Reservoir, one and a half miles west-by-south of Capelrig. The secret position of the third point remains a mystery, but he who discovers it and digs in the centre of the triangle shall find a treasure fit to maintain a king. This has never been disproved.

In 1567 the Temple lands of Renfrewshire were acquired by Bryce Semple of

Capelrig House seen during the construction of Eastwood High School which opened in Newton Mearns in 1964.

Beltrees, from whom Capelrig later passed to the Muirs of Caldwell. After the Restoration in 1660, the land of Covenanters was confiscated. One of their leaders was William Muir, the owner of Capelrig, who fled to Holland. His estates were granted to General Thomas Dalziel of Binns [an ancestor of Tam Dalziel MP], commander of the royal forces at Rullian Green, for successfully persecuting the Covenanters.

Robert Barclay bought Capelrig in 1765, and in 1769 built Capelrig House, 'a neat handsome house, three stories high, rustic cornered with eleven steps of a stone stair up to the front door'. When he died the estate fell to his niece, who married into the Brown family.

The watch tower near Patterton station was known as Spy House and was built by George Brown in the late eighteenth century so that guests at Capelrig could watch the coursing of hounds (hare hunting with dogs).

Eastwood High School was built as part of Renfrewshire's reorganisation of secondary schooling in the district into a two-tier system. Younger secondary pupils attended Woodfarm and Williamwood High Schools and older pupils the new Eastwood. This system, which was comprehensive only in S1 and S2 and selective thereafter, was superseded by the present all-through secondary schools in the late 1970s. Nowadays post-primary children in Newton Mearns attend Eastwood or Mearns Castle non-denominational high schools or travel to St Ninian's Roman Catholic high school in Eastwood Park (formerly Lord Weir's estate). The science wing of Eastwood High School was destroyed by fire in 1984, but the laboratories were rebuilt in time for the school's jubilee celebrations in 1987.

Much changed in and around the big houses of Mearns during the twentieth century. At the beginning of the twenty-first century, with children of school-age numbering thousands rather than a few hundred, gone too are the days of the kind of largesse recorded in Mearns School's log for 22 June 1911:

To honour the Coronation of King George V and Queen Mary, all Mearns school-children received a medal from Mrs Marshall of Crookfur and a silver sixpence from the Misses Anderson of Hazeldean.

After the medals were presented, led by a piper, the children marched through the village, first to a cinematographic exhibition in the new Church Hall [now the Glasgow New Synagogue Centre] and then to games and races in Gilmour's fields. Each child was given a pie and milk and proceedings closed with all singing the National Anthem.

Chapter 8

New Faces . . . and New Places

Like all Scottish places with any aspirations to a history, Mearns has its castle. The following two descriptions come from the *Statistical Accounts* of 1796 and 1842:

> The only antiquity here is the Castle of Mearns. It is a large square tower, situated on a rocky eminence and commanding an extensive and beautiful prospect. It is not known when it was built. It is supposed to be several hundred years old and to have been used as a place of defence. It was surrounded by a strong wall and the entrance was secured by a draw-bridge. It is now, however, greatly dismantled and out of repair, the family of Blackhall, to whom it belongs, having their residence at Ardgowan.

> An ancient square tower is still pointed out, which passes under the name of the Old Castle of Mearns. This was formerly the chief seat of the Maxwells. It has lately been roofed in and is surmounted with a flagstaff. The roof is so contrived that, being invisible from without, it does not disfigure the building. On a late occasion, the ancient echoes of the antique warlike fortalice were awaked after a sleep of centuries to the voice of music and the nimble cadence of the 'light fantastic toe'.

In 1972 the former castle was incorporated into Maxwell Mearns Parish Church of Scotland (although the castle is now unsafe and unused). This church carried the name Maxwell from its former parish in the Kingston district of Glasgow, where it closed in the 1960s after a ministry of over 100 years. Coincidentally, Maxwell is the first recorded name in the history of Mearns Castle. On 15 March 1449 King James II granted Herbert, first Lord Maxwell of Caerlaverock and Mearns, a licence

> to big [i.e. build] a castle or fortalice on the Baronie of Mearns, to surround it with strong walls and ditches, to strengthen it with iron gates, and to erect on top of it all warlike apparatus necessary for its defence.

These were indeed turbulent times. The south, west, and north walls are eight feet thick, and the east ten feet as the position was more vulnerable from attack from that direction. The landfall to the north, west and south offered natural defence and the east was further protected by a ditch spanned by a drawbridge. The castle is 45 feet high with three floors, and no evidence exists of its ever having been taken.

The main entrance was an arched doorway eleven feet up the east wall, presumably reached by a moveable wooden staircase of some sort. An iron-studded door below this at ground level led into a dungeon-like area, cold enough for salted carcasses to be stored in during winter. The upper floors were heated by log fires. A minstrels' gallery suggests festivities – perhaps when, as legend has it, Mary, Queen of Scots and Henry, Lord Darnley, visited the castle prior to the Battle of Langside. On old maps the hillock to the east of the castle is called King Harry's Knowe.

Later, conventicles occasionally took place in the castle but these ceased when it was occupied by dragoons, who were garrisoned there to patrol the Mearns, Eaglesham and Fenwick moors and disperse Covenanting worshippers who might gather there. (The moors were common land, and hence no landowner would have been punished if a conventicle was discovered taking place there.) The castle changed ownership several times and was gradually neglected – as reported in the first *Statistical Account*.

Church or ruin, the castle has always been a local vantage point. When Caleb of the *Citizen* met Robert Pollok's brother David at Waterfoot to be escorted up the valley of the Earn to the Pollok family home at Moorhouse, the two men made a detour to survey the countryside from the top of the castle. Judging from the eloquence of his description, Caleb found the detour worthwhile:

> We now ascend to the battlements of the tower from which we obtain a splendid prospect of the surrounding country. In the south are the dreary moors of Eaglesham, swelling upward to Ballygeich, and fretted with numerous flocks and herds. Westward, amidst a very sea of verdant knolls, clumps of woods and yellow fields, are Mearns Kirk and the Newton, with Dod Hill and Neilston Pad in the distance. To the north and east is the great valley of the Clyde, studded with towns, villages, and mansions, while the Renfrewshire, Kilpatrick, and Campsie Hills rise proudly beyond and the blue mountains of the Gael are faintly visible on the misty horizon.
>
> Beautiful indeed is the wavy bosom of the Mearns, as it lies outspread before us in the warm sunshine of the autumn noon. Merry groups are busy in the fields and the blue smoke curling over cottage and hall gives pleasant indication of happy hearths.

Over 100 years later Mearns Kirk and the hills still form part of the distant view, but the 'merry groups' in the foreground now comprise young people and adults en route to and from classes and activities in Mearns Castle High School, adjacent to Maxwell Mearns Church.

The change in character of Mearns dates from the 1930s when 1,600 new houses were built, 300 by Renfrew County Council south-west of the village and 1,300 privately south-east and east. Further changes were arrested, of course, when building ceased throughout the Second World War and its aftermath. Before the war the population had doubled from the 1931 census figure of 4,635 but remained under 10,000 until housebuilding resumed in the late 1950s, when the main private builders were Mactaggart & Mickel in Broom Estate and east of Mearns Road, and John Lawrence between Ayr Road and Stewarton Road. The present population of the five wards of Mearns, Crookfur, Broom, Kirkhill and

Greenfarm, based on the 2001 census, is 23,413. This represents an increase of 16 per cent on the 1991 figure of 20,149. However, it is worth noting that 82 per cent of all population growth in East Renfrewshire is contained in these wards, making Mearns a very popular place to live. Almost the only open land remaining between Mearns and the adjacent suburbs of Thornliebank, Giffnock and Clarkston is the green belt formed by Rouken Glen Park, Whitecraigs Golf Club and Cathcart Castle Golf Club.

Golf courses account for much of 'green' Mearns: there are three to the north (the two already mentioned and a third beside Rouken Glen Park at Deaconsbank); and three to the south – East Renfrewshire, Eastwood and Bonnyton. The Eastwood Club moved from Giffnock to its present moorland course between the wars when houses were built at Orchard Park. After the Second World War, when many clubs did not admit Jewish members (a practice that seems extraordinary today), the Jewish community bought the public course on Bonnyton Moor and founded their own club (which exercises no exclusions). Many conifers were planted, giving some shelter to the fairways and enhancing the bare moorland without obscuring the spectacular views – west and south to the Firth of Clyde and Arran; north across the city to the Campsie Fells, Kilpatrick Hills and Ben Lomond beyond.

Most Jewish immigrants to Glasgow originally lived in the Gorbals, then gradually moved southwards into Shawlands, Langside, Giffnock, Clarkston and Newton Mearns. The Star of David symbol on Ayr Road, opposite the former Mearns Primary School, identifies one of Mearns's two synagogues, recently refurbished and extended. The modern building behind it (entered from Larchfield Avenue) is one of Glasgow's seven orthodox synagogues. 1879 saw the opening of the first synagogue in Scotland – at Garnethill – a gathering-place for the 700 Jews who then lived in Glasgow. They were mostly merchants and businessmen of German and Dutch origin. From the turn of the twentieth century, however, to escape growing restrictions in Tsarist Russia and its empire in the Ukraine, Lithuania, Latvia and Poland, thousands of Jewish refugees moved westwards seeking freedom to carry on their businesses, educate their children, and practise their religion. By 1930 four million Jews had left Eastern Europe, the majority of whom travelled to the Americas and to Palestine. Many who fled from Nazi Germany settled in the United Kingdom and in 1935 Glasgow's Jewish population was estimated at 15,000. Emigration to Israel has since reduced this total, but of the remaining 10,000 many are among the new faces of Newton Mearns. In 2003 the effects of globalisation have not passed Mearns by, and the area is fast becoming even more multicultural.

The considerable increase in population from the second half of the last century onwards has not been the result of the coming of new industry. Mearns has become almost entirely residential, and to live and to work here nowadays is the exception rather than the rule, a reversal of the pattern of earlier days. Only one manufacturing enterprise of any size, Coats Barbour Ltd., is operational. The company, which employs about 200 people, is involved in the dye processing of industrial threads and orders are received from all over the world. UK customers include Next, Marks & Spencer and the British army and navy. Threads dyed at Newton Mearns were used in the costumes in the 2002 film *Harry Potter and the Chamber of Secrets*. The works' metal-faced chimney is the only conspicuous industrial landmark in the Mearns area. A century ago bleaching, printing and dyeing works also operated at Hazelden, Broom and the Tofts – these were good locations for such works because of the damp air and abundant supply of soft water.

In the early 1900s the Tofts company built larger works at Netherplace and by the thirties the only reminder of their original location was the manager's house, Tofts House. It still

survives, surrounded by trees and the many houses of Rodger and Lambie Avenues. The fortunes of this Netherplace cloth finishing firm – Wallace & Company, then Tootal, now Coats Barbour – have fluctuated considerably, and from 1980 to 1986 the works were closed after running down for several years. It's hard to believe now that at one time there were rows of workers' cottages at both Netherplace and Tofts. The cottages at Tofts were across from and behind Greenside in the valley below St Cadoc's Primary School, named after an ancient British saint of the sixth century.

This choice of a British saint from the old Celtic form of Christianity for a church and school in Mearns fits well with theories about the origin of the name Mearns itself. The Revd MacKellar opened his *New Statistical Account* thus:

> The name of this Parish first appears in authentic form in the Chartulary of Glasgow, and in Prynne, as far back as the year 1296 – the eventful period when Edward I of England made his celebrated attempt to wrest from the hands of Scotsmen their rights and privileges and to annex Scotland's ancient crown and sceptre permanently to the throne of England. The power of Edward's arms was felt and acknowledged throughout the better portion of the Lowlands of Scotland, and many a wealthy ecclesiastic and proud noble were constrained to bow the neck and swear fealty to the common enemy. Among the many victims to the power of England, John Petit of the MEIRNES is mentioned in the records of the times as one of the barons of the day who swore fealty to Edward I.
>
> The spelling of the name of this parish, like all other ancient names, varies exceedingly . . . the oldest form is MEIRNES, as above, but it is also frequently styled MERNES, MEARNIS, MEIRNES, and MORNESS.

Opposite upper:
Netherplace works. The pond was constructed in the mid-1850s.

Opposite lower:
Workers from Wallace & Co. of Netherplace. A group of women can be seen outside the hostel known as the 'woman house'. Netherplace House is in the background.

Jim Carvel at Wallace & Co., Netherplace, in the mid-1960s, with a 250 yard bale of terylene net.

O'Brien in his Word-Book derives the modern name MEARNS from the British MAERONAS – a name exactly descriptive of this parish: 'a district inhabited by herdsmen'. . . . this parish has ever been distinguished as a district for pasturage and at the present day the produce of the dairy . . . obtains a ready and favourite market in the neighbouring city of Glasgow.

Perhaps originally the name was not applied to any particular place but was a general appellation applicable to an indefinite extent of pastoral country. This in later times took the names of the Kirk Towns, or more conspicuous villages with which the several places composing it were respectively connected. That somewhat extensive district lying between the rivers Dee and North Esk . . . is still occasionally known by the appellation of 'the Mearns'.

A view similar to O'Brien's is offered by Boyd Scott in *Old Days and Ways in Newton Mearns*. He associates the name with the ancient British princes of Strathclyde, among whose land officers one rank was designated Maer, meaning steward of a Maeroni. Boyd Scott goes on to propose that this could later have been anglicised as Mearns.

Whatever significance may attach to the word Mearns one thing is certain – the word Newton has long lost any literal meaning. Newton Mearns, new as much of it is, has a very long history. The identity of the area is, however, swiftly changing as more and more houses are built and more and more families settle.

Mearns Castle.

Further reading

The books listed below were used by the authors during their research. None of them is available from Stenlake Publishing. Those interested in finding out more are advised to contact their local bookshop or reference library.

1775, John Howie, *The Scots Worthies*
1791–99, *Statistical Account of Scotland*
1823, Robert Pollok, *Tales of the Covenanters*
1827, Robert Pollok, *The Course of Time*
1834–45, *New Statistical Account of Scotland*
1842, *Recreations of Christopher North*
1846, David Pollok, *Life of Robert Pollok*
1854, Caleb, *Rambles Round Glasgow*
1919, Mearns Cattle Show Programme
1920, T. C. F. Brotchie, *Tramways Guide*
1939, A. Boyd Scott, *Old Days and Ways in Newton Mearns*
1939, J. A. Strang, *A History of Mearns Parish* (3 volumes, bound typescript)
1941, Hansard, Volumes 371 and 372
1944–62, *Third Statistical Account of Scotland*
1949, Mearnskirk and Peter Pan: Souvenir Brochure
1950, Churchill, *The Second World War*
1955, Mearnskirk Hospital 1930–1955: Pictorial Album
1964, Eden, *Memoirs: The Reckoning*
1969, Year Book of Mearns Horticultural Society
1969, Eastwood School Magazine
1970, Henry Hay, *Newton Mearns Past and Present*
1971, James Douglas-Hamilton, *Motive for a Mission*
1976, Royal Observer Corps, *Hess Affair; May 10, 1941*
1976, Mearns School Centenary Magazine
1979, Belmont House School Golden Jubilee Magazine
1980, Mearnskirk Hospital Golden Jubilee Pictorial Album
1982, *Twelve Centuries of Christian Witness at Mearns Parish Church*
1984, C. Hutt and H. Kaplan, *A Scottish Shtetl*
1986, M. Glickman, *The Glasgow Jewish Community*
1988, Eastwood District Libraries, *Fairest Parish – A History of Mearns*
1989, Dr Thomas C. Welsh, *Eastwood District: History and Heritage*
1990, ed. S. D. Slater & D. A. Dow, *The Victoria Infirmary of Glasgow 1890–1990*

Main Street facing north.
The two-storey building in the right foreground was the first manse of the Secession Church.